A Birdfinding Guide To The Calgary Region

D1596236

Edited by

Joan F. McDonald

Calgary Field Naturalists' Society

Calgary Field Naturalists' Society,
P.O. Box 981,
Calgary,
Alberta, T2P 2K4.

Canadian Cataloguing in Publication Data

Main entry under title:
A Birdfinding guide to the Calgary region

   Includes index,
   ISBN 0-921224-05-2

   1. Bird watching—Alberta—Calgary Region.
2. Birds—Alberta—Calgary Region.   I.
McDonald, Joan F. (Joan Frances).   II.
Calgary Field Naturalists' Society.
QL685.5.A4B57 1993   598'.07234712338
                        C93-091336-1

Front Cover:	Yellow-headed Blackbird, photo by Frans Brouwers
Back Cover:	Spruce Grouse, photo by Wayne W. Smith

Printed in Canada on oxygen bleached, acid-free, recycled paper.

Contents

Introduction 2

Possible Wildlife Hazards 4

A Birders' Code of Ethics 6

Site Guides:

Section A: The City of Calgary
A-1 Inglewood Bird Sanctuary 8
A-2 Fish Creek Provincial Park 11
A-3 Lowery Gardens and The Douglas Fir Trail 15
A-4 Bowness Park 18
A-5 Nose Hill Park 21
A-6 Glenmore Reservoir and The Weaselhead
 Natural Area 24
A-7 The University of Calgary Campus 28
A-8 Winter Birding Along The Bow River 33

Section B: The Prairies
B-1 Shepard Sloughs, Dalemead Reservoir and
 Wyndham-Carseland Provincial Park 39
B-2 Sadler's Slough 44
B-3 Eagle Lake 46
B-4 Namaka Lake 49
B-5 McElroy Slough Driving Route 51
B-6 The Irricana Area and Bruce Lake Driving Route 54
B-7 The Drumheller Area 59
B-8 Frank Lake 64
B-9 McGregor Lake 67

Section C: The Foothills
C-1 Big Hill Springs Provincial Park 72
C-2 Grand Valley Road/Springbank Raptor Route 75
C-3 The Water Valley Area 78
C-4 The Forestry Trunk Road 83
C-5 The Sheep River Valley 86

C-6   Brown-Lowery Recreation Area   91
C-7   Bow Valley Provincial Park   94
C-8   Lac Des Arcs   98
C-9   Smith-Dorrien/Spray Trail   99
C-10 Sibbald Creek Trail   103
C-11 The Kananaskis Valley   107
C-12 The Highwood Valley   115

Section D: Banff National Park
D-1   Cave and Basin Marsh   121
D-2   Fenland Trail and Vermilion Lakes Drive   124
D-3   Johnston Canyon   127
D-4   Muleshoe Picnic Area   129
D-5   Sunshine Meadows   130
D-6   The Lake Louise Area   134

Section E: Brooks and the Eastern Irrigation District
E-1   Wolf Lake and Crawling Valley Reservoir   140
E-2   Dinosaur Provincial Park   143
E-3   Kinbrook Island Provincial Park and Lake Newell   148
E-4   The Brooks Area   151

Species Locator   159

Seasonal Status and Abundance Chart   169

Rarely-Observed Species   181

Reporting of Bird Sightings   186

Useful Books   189

Index   191

Acknowledgements

Birdfinding guides are, by their very nature, highly specialized books requiring the expert knowledge and efforts of many people to produce. This book has been made possible through the help and enthusiasm of the following and their contributions are gratefully acknowledged.

The book was put together with the assistance of an editorial team consisting of Ross Dickson, Dave Elphinstone, Malcolm McDonald, Andrew Slater and Richard Thomas. As well as reviewing the text, the team also spent many long evenings fortified by many cups of tea and muffins compiling the Species Locator and the Seasonal Status and Abundance Chart and these parts of the book represent a consensus of their experience and opinions. Ross Dickson and Richard Thomas compiled the Rarely-Observed Species list; the maps and the graphics for the Seasonal Status and Abundance Chart were prepared by Malcolm McDonald.

The text of each birding location or route was written by, or with the aid of, the individuals whose names appear at the end of each contribution. Portions of the book were reviewed by the following and their comments and suggestions enhanced the final text: Jamey Podlubny, Bill Wilson, Wayne Smith, Harold Pinel, Bruce Anderson and Louis Guillemette. Ian Halladay read the first draft and made suggestions for its improvement.

The groundwork for parts of the book was laid by earlier members of the Calgary Field Naturalists' Society and the contributions of Ian Halladay, Jack Steeves and Al Wiseley are particularly acknowledged.

Finally, the invaluable assistance provided by TransAlta Utilities Corporation is acknowledged. Dave Brinsmead and Wayne St. Amour arranged for digitizing the maps, conversion of the text computer files, and for running off draft copies of the book in preparation for printing.

Joan McDonald

Introduction

The city of Calgary straddles the Bow River as it emerges from the foothills of the Rocky Mountains on the northwestern edge of the Great Plains. This guide is an introduction to the birding possibilities of what we have termed the "Calgary Region" which is essentially the area that can be comfortably covered in a full day's outing from the city. The Calgary Region contains more varied bird habitats and ranges than almost any other location in Canada. Within a day's drive it is possible to visit alpine, subalpine and foothills habitats, boreal forest, muskeg, aspen parkland, riverine forest, natural grasslands, eroded badlands, seasonal sloughs, wetlands and lakes. This great diversity of natural environments, coupled with the Region's location in the overlap zone between "western" and "eastern" breeding species ensures that the Calgary Region has much to offer both local and visiting birders. Since 1975, 350 species have been recorded within the Region and are dealt with in this guide; 297 of them are deemed to be of regular occurrence.

The book has three major elements. The first, the main body of the text, describes the birding locations. For convenience, the Region has been divided into five sections which roughly approximate discrete geographic areas. Within each section the birding locations are presented as either descriptions of a specific locale, such as a park, or as detailed driving routes. The second part, the "Species Locator", is designed to aid birders in identifying the best locations to look for certain species. These species are either those considered to be regional specialties, or ones that less experienced birders may have difficulty in finding. The third part, the "Seasonal Status and Abundance Chart", shows in graphic form the optimal times for looking.

The maps provided contain sufficient information to be used alone but it is recommended that they be used in conjunction with the official Alberta Road Map. This is published by Alberta Tourism and can be obtained from any Travel Alberta Information Centre or by writing to: Alberta Tourism, Box 2500, Edmonton, Alberta, T5J 2Z4 (1-800-661-8888). The preferred topographic maps for southern Alberta are the 1:250,000 series published by Alberta Forestry, Lands and Wildlife as these are the most up-to-date.

The City of Calgary operates a Wildlife Information Line and Bird Alert: (403) 237–8821. This number is staffed between 8:00 a.m. and 4:00 p.m. weekdays. At other times there is a recorded message giving the birding highlights of the Calgary Region. A steady supply of information is required for the birding hotline to function properly. If you have up-to–date information on noteworthy species, call the hotline during office hours.

Possible Wildlife Hazards

Bears, Moose, Elk etc. The foothill and mountain regions of southern Alberta are blessed with an abundant and varied mammalian fauna. When hiking in wilderness areas, birders should have an understanding of the patterns of animal behaviour and keep in mind that the onus of preventing an unexpected wildlife encounter rests with themselves. When learning birding techniques, we are encouraged to act quietly and to blend in with our surroundings. In wilderness areas, however, the key to safety is to remain alert and to advertise one's presence through noise. Black Bears are fairly common in almost any habitat below tree line, particularly in montane woodland. Grizzly Bears are less common but may occur in any mountain environment. Bears can be active between March and early November. Be especially alert in the vicinity of creeks, where the noise of the water may mask the sound of one's approach. Other large mammals to be aware of are Moose and Elk with young, and male Moose, Elk and deer during the rut.

Ticks Wood ticks look like small, flat, slow moving apple seeds. They occur in grassy areas where small mammals, such as ground squirrels, are common. On the eastern slopes of the Rocky Mountains wood ticks can be the carriers of a disease known as Rocky Mountain spotted fever. When hiking in the foothills and mountains of southern Alberta between April and the end of June, birders should observe the following precautions. Dress sensibly, covering as much of your body as possible; tuck your pant legs into your socks. Light coloured clothing is best as ticks are more easily seen against it and can be picked off. Insect repellent containing a high concentration of DEET, applied to socks and pant legs, may discourage ticks. Check yourself thoroughly as soon as you arrive home. Any ticks you can remove should be flushed down the toilet. Do not handle crushed ticks as this can lead to infection. If you find you have an unwelcome guest firmly attached by its mouthparts, consult a physician before attempting any home remedies.

Rattlesnakes The Prairie race of the Western Rattlesnake inhabits the arid short-grass prairie regions of southeastern Alberta and southwestern Saskatchewan. Within this area it is generally confined to the slopes of river valleys, though it may move out beyond these during the summer. With a common sense approach, rattlesnakes should not pose a hazard to birders. Try to keep to cleared pathways; do not walk through brush or long grass. Check the other side before stepping over rocks or logs. Never reach into crevices or under rocks or logs. Check the surroundings before sitting down.

Mosquitoes The reservoirs, sloughs, marshes and irrigation ditches of southern Alberta, beloved by birders for their shorebirds and water-fowl, are also extremely attractive to mosquitoes as breeding grounds. Unless you are of a particularly stoic disposition, carry a reliable insect repellent between May and September.

A Birder's Code Of Ethics

Birding is an absorbing and extremely satisfying pastime for a growing number of people. In the excitement of finding something unusual, or in adding a new species to one's life list, it is often easy to forget the basic ground rules.

1. **The primary concern of every birder should be the welfare of the birds and the protection of the habitat which supports them.**

   When observing or photographing birds keep disturbance to a minimum; never repeatedly flush a bird.

   Never disturb a nest in any way, or remove vegetation from around a nest site.

   Keep the use of tape recordings to a minimum, especially during the nesting season.

   Always observe nesting colonies from a distance—use a scope.

   Never enter a wetland during the nesting season.

   Always observe raptor nests from a distance—Ferruginous Hawks, in particular, may abandon the nest if disturbed while incubating.

   Do not disturb flightless waterfowl during the moulting season.

2. **Respect private property.**

   To avoid trespassing, always obtain permission before birding on private land.

   Whenever possible keep to paths and roadways; never cross growing crops.

   Do not cause disturbance to livestock.

   Leave all gates exactly as you found them.

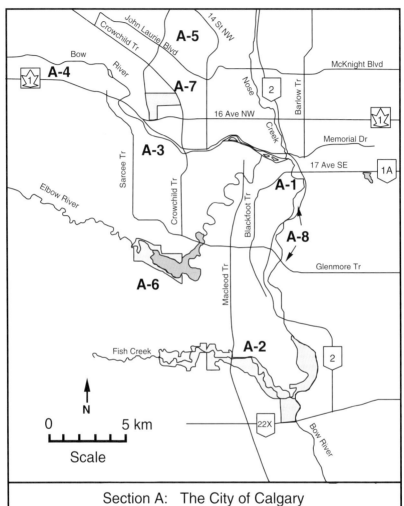

Section A: The City of Calgary

A-1   Inglewood Bird Sanctuary
A-2   Fish Creek Provincial Park
A-3   Lowery Gardens and The Douglas Fir Trail
A-4   Bowness Park
A-5   Nose Hill Park
A-6   Glenmore Reservoir and The Weaselhead Natural Area
A-7   The University of Calgary Campus
A-8   Winter Birding Along The Bow River

A-1 Inglewood Bird Sanctuary

The Inglewood Bird Sanctuary is a city park that has been designated a Natural Area and a federal migratory bird sanctuary. It consists of approximately 34 hectares of riverine woodland in an otherwise mostly industrial setting. This area usually produces the city's finest concentrations of warblers during fall migration, plus it is the best location in Calgary for finding uncommon species of gull in spring and late fall.

To reach the Sanctuary, drive east on 9 Ave SE and turn south on Sanctuary Road to the parking lot. (From the Deerfoot Trail, take the Blackfoot Trail westbound exit to 19 St SE, then turn left from this onto 9 Ave.) The Bow River Pathway skirts the boundary of the Sanctuary, providing pedestrian and bicycle access to the area as well. Inglewood is open from dawn to dusk every day of the year. The Colonel Walker house, located near the entrance, is a provincially designated historic site which was built in 1910. It is currently used by Sanctuary staff as an office area and classroom space for a variety of natural history courses and programs. A bird checklist may be obtained here during working hours.

The Sanctuary has approximately 2.5 km of wood chip pathways. A compacted gravel trail, accessible to wheelchairs, runs along the western shore of the lagoon between the south bridge and the river. To help protect this special place, please stay on the pathways.

A walk through the Sanctuary will reveal three flood terraces, or levels. The upper terrace is covered mainly by disturbed grassland, cultivated trees and shrubs; the Walker house is situated upon it. The middle terrace is dominated by Balsam Poplar trees, while the lowest terrace is an area that is often flooded and is dominated by willow. The most prominent feature of the landscape at Inglewood is the lagoon in the centre of the area. This natural off-channel of the Bow River was dredged, dammed and expanded in the past to produce its present shape. Natural springs within the Sanctuary have been warm enough to keep water channels partially open in winter, assisted by the movement of thousands of Mallards. However, due to changes in these springs in recent years, only the northern end of the lagoon now remains open in winter.

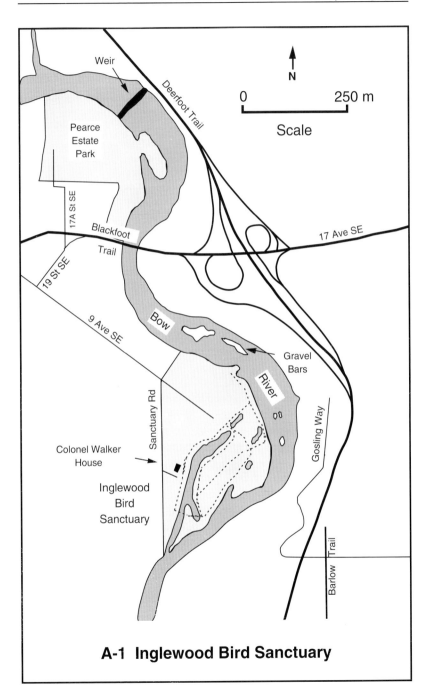

A-1 Inglewood Bird Sanctuary

The chance to see birds at the Sanctuary changes dramatically from season to season. In May, small numbers of eastern and western warblers can be observed, together with summer residents such as American Kestrel, Northern Flicker, Western Wood-Pewee, Least Flycatcher, Eastern Kingbird and Northern (Baltimore) Oriole. Of the warblers, only the Yellow nests regularly.

By far the most opportune time to watch for migrant songbirds is from the beginning of August until the end of September. On exceptionally good days up to twenty species of warblers may be found by the observant birder. Warblers to watch for include: Tennessee, Orange-crowned, Yellow, Chestnut-sided, Magnolia, Cape May, Yellow-rumped, Townsend's, Black-throated Green, Palm, Bay-breasted, Blackpoll, Black-and–white, American Redstart, MacGillivray's, Common Yellowthroat, Wilson's and Canada. Warblers that have been recorded on only a few occasions at Inglewood include Nashville, Northern Parula, Black-throated Blue, Black-throated Gray and Yellow-breasted Chat. Other species to watch for at this time include flycatchers, nuthatches, kinglets, and Warbling and Red-eyed Vireos. Accipiters, especially Sharp-shinneds, are attracted by these flocks of migrating passerines. A first for the province was a Blue-gray Gnatcatcher that showed up in the fall of 1988 and again in 1989.

In winter, thousands of Mallards and the tame Black-capped Chickadees are the most visible residents. White-breasted Nuthatches have become regular winter residents as well. Watch for Bald Eagles—these prey on sick waterfowl. A Great Horned Owl may be encountered on its day-time perch.

In early spring and late fall many local birders watch the Bow River at Inglewood for regular migrants and unexpected rarities. The most productive area is the series of gravel bars towards the northern end. Uncommon gulls recorded here include Mew, Thayer's, Iceland, Glaucous-winged and Glaucous. A Lesser Black-backed Gull, a first for the province, was observed here both in the spring and fall of 1989. Interesting ducks to watch for include Harlequin, Common and Barrow's Goldeneyes, and all three Mergansers. Descendents of a small introduced population of Wood Ducks nest in the old Balsam Poplars—the only place in southern Alberta where this species can be reliably found. In winter they move out onto the Bow River.

The Sanctuary has washrooms; facilities for the disabled are available from April to September inclusive. Drinking water must be brought in by the visitor as the tap water is unpalatable. For more information phone the Sanctuary office at 269–6688.

DAVE ELPHINSTONE

A-2 Fish Creek Provincial Park

Fish Creek Provincial Park is the largest park in Calgary. Lying in a broad, deep valley it is 19 kilometres from Mallard Point at the eastern end to Shannon Terrace in the west. There are two reasons why the park is an important area for birders: the diversity of habitats attracts a wide variety of breeding species, plus it is one of the best winter birding locations.

Macleod Trail effectively divides the park in two. Key birding access points for the western section are the following parking areas: **Votier's Flats** (reached from the southern end of Elbow Drive); **Bebo Grove** (from 24 St SW); and **Shannon Terrace** (from 37 St SW). Birding access points for the eastern portion of the park are the **Bankside, Burnsmead** and **Hull's Wood** parking areas (reached from Bow Bottom Trail); and Mallard Point (from Canyon Meadows Drive).

Fish Creek Provincial Park is heavily used for recreational purposes— birders should avoid weekends, if possible; if not, go early in the morning. Unfortunately, all of the above access points are gated until 8:00 a.m., preventing vehicular access. Birders arriving prior to this may park in the adjacent residential areas and walk in.

The park Visitor Centre is reached from the Bow Bottom Trail access point; detailed trail maps of the park can be obtained here. Many of the paved trails are heavily used by cyclists. Caution should be exercised when birding from these trails, especially at blind corners.

The eastern portion of the park (Macleod Trail to the Bow River) is comprised mainly of grassland and open deciduous woodland. In the

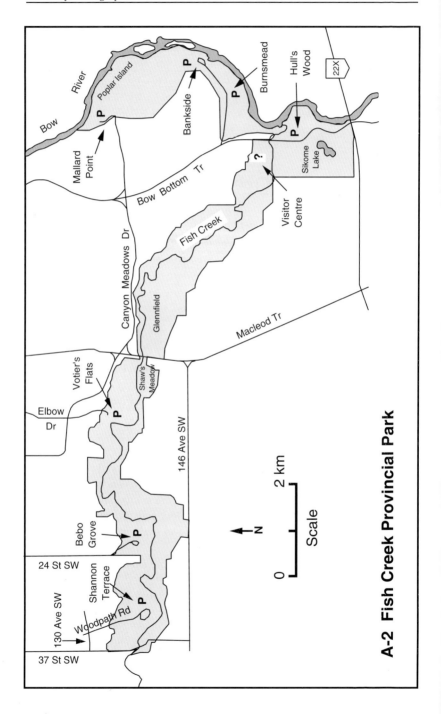

A-2 Fish Creek Provincial Park

western segment, the Votier's Flats area has a combination of grass-
land, deciduous woodland, riverine willow and White Spruce growth.
White Spruce forms the dominant vegetation from Bebo Grove to
Shannon Terrace.

Many open woodland species will be found along the trails between
Votier's Flats and **Bebo Grove** (approx. 4.5 km one way) in late May
and early June. These include: Downy and Hairy Woodpeckers; North-
ern Flicker; Western Wood-Pewee; Least Flycatcher; Eastern Kingbird;
House Wren; Cedar Waxwing; Warbling and Red-eyed Vireos;
Tennessee and Yellow Warblers; possibly Ovenbird; and Northern
Oriole. This is also one of the best locations within Calgary for finding
Yellow-bellied Sapsucker. Along the creek, watch for Great Blue Heron,
Blue-winged Teal, American Wigeon, Common Merganser, Spotted
Sandpiper and Belted Kingfisher. At this time of year you may also see
a Solitary Sandpiper. Dusky Flycatcher and Eastern Phoebe are often
seen along the creek; Sora and Common Yellowthroat inhabit the
marshy margins of the area. Five species of swallow (Tree, Northern
Rough-winged, Bank, Cliff and Barn) may be seen on this walk.

In the grasslands and nearby brushy areas, watch for Ring-necked
Pheasant, Clay-colored Sparrow which is abundant here, and Savannah Sparrow. Both Chipping and Lincoln's Sparrows occur here as
well, but with Chipping found closer to wooded areas and Lincoln's
closer to wetter areas. Note also that this area is one of the most reliable in the city for finding Veery, Gray Catbird and White-throated
Sparrow at this time of year. Watch for catbirds in areas of thick brush
along the creek. Look for Veery and White-throated Sparrow in areas
of deciduous growth with a fairly dense understory, particularly
between Votier's Flats and Bebo Grove. Le Conte's Sparrow is possible in grassy areas, especially just east of the 24 St parking area,
Shaw's Meadow, and the moister parts of the Glennfield area.

A good number and variety of raptors should be seen. Both Swainson's and Red-tailed Hawks can be seen in the Votier's Flats area;
American Kestrel is a common nester in both the eastern and western
parts of the park. Watch for accipiters in the western end, as this is
very good habitat for them. Great Horned Owl is a common nesting
predator, and Fish Creek is the only area within city limits where
Barred Owl has been reported recently, with a nest being recorded in
the early 1980s and again in 1989.

Prairie Falcon used to nest in the Raven Rocks area (between Votier's Flats and Shannon Terrace) prior to residential development near the sandstone cliffs. An attempt was made to re-establish this species by means of a "hacking" program in the 1980s. This met with little success, however, and has been discontinued.

The trails between **Bebo Grove** and **Shannon Terrace** (1.3 km) should furnish most of the species indigenous to the coniferous forest of the Calgary area. A productive half-day walk should produce Ruffed Grouse, Boreal Chickadee, Red-breasted Nuthatch, Ruby-crowned Kinglet, Western Tanager, Purple Finch and Pine Siskin. Watch for Rose-breasted Grosbeak also, as it is seen here regularly. Both Olive-sided and Western Flycatchers are regularly sighted in this area. Olive-sided Flycatcher is a confirmed nester, and Western has been seen annually near the steep creek bank, immediately south of the Shannon Terrace Environmental Centre. Gray Jay may be found throughout the year and Blue Jay, once very rare in Calgary, is now a common nester.

Bebo Grove and Shannon Terrace are also prime winter birding areas. At this season watch for Northern Goshawk; Three-toed and Pileated Woodpeckers; Common Raven; Mountain and Boreal Chickadees; Dark-eyed Junco (in early and late winter); and Common Redpoll. This is also one of the best winter "owling" spots within the city, with Great Horned often seen and Northern Pygmy and Northern Saw-whet being reported occasionally. American Dipper can sometimes be found where there is open water.

The other productive winter birding area in Fish Creek Provincial Park is along the Bow River, in the eastern sector. Park at either **Mallard Point, Bankside, Burnsmead** or **Hull's Wood** parking areas and walk the trails along the river. Mallard will be the most common species but Canada Goose, Common Goldeneye and Common Merganser overwinter in some numbers. Watch also for uncommon stragglers such as Northern Pintail, Gadwall, American Wigeon, Redhead and Killdeer. At least one Bald Eagle should be observed; Gyrfalcon and Northern Goshawk have been seen here as well. Some unusual winter records in this area in recent years include a Trumpeter Swan which overwintered in 1985–86, a female Red-winged Blackbird in January, 1988 and a flock of 19 Brewer's Blackbirds in January, 1989.

In summer, watch for Common and Black Terns along the Bow River and Cliff Swallows nesting under the Hwy 22X bridge.

TERRY KOROLYK

A-3 Lowery Gardens and The Douglas Fir Trail

The mountain-like vegetation of the Douglas Fir Trail and riparian woodland of Lowery Gardens at the eastern end of Edworthy Park help to concentrate a locally unique mixture of bird species. Stretching along the south side of the Bow River in northwest Calgary the area contains a steep north-facing escarpment, grasslands, floodplain and ravines just minutes from downtown.

From the north, the Douglas Fir Trail can be accessed by parking at the Harry Boothman pedestrian bridge, near the intersection of 16 Ave NW (Trans-Canada Highway) and Bowness Road. Follow the footpath across the bridge and the railway, and then turn left (east) towards the conifers. Visitors from the southwest can find parking areas by leaving Bow Trail at 45 St SW and turning west at Spruce Drive, which then enters Edworthy Park. Parking is available at the Pumphouse Theatre, at the west end of 9 Ave SW, for those who wish to visit Lowery Gardens from the east side. An alternative parking area, closer to Lowery Gardens, can be reached by following 10 Ave west, under the Crowchild Trail bridge, to its very end, then turning right along the lane behind the first row of commercial buildings and proceeding slowly, on a rough track that can be muddy, to a parking area on the south side of the railway tracks.

The 1.5 km **Douglas Fir Trail** is an occasionally steep pathway along the escarpment. The area contains one of the most easterly stands of Douglas Fir in Alberta; some of the trees are more than 400 years old. This is an excellent area for finding Blue Jay; Boreal and Mountain Chickadees; both Golden- and Ruby-crowned Kinglets; Veery; and Yellow-rumped Warbler. To bird this area effectively during migration, find an open area in the forest (especially with a trickle of water)

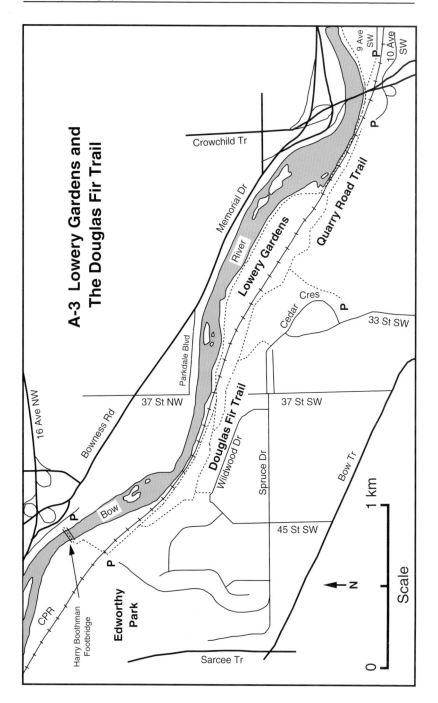

A-3 Lowery Gardens and
The Douglas Fir Trail

and wait there. You can often look across or down on mixed flocks of warblers (including Townsend's), Western Tanager and Rose-breasted Grosbeak. In winter, this area may host Northern Goshawk, Brown Creeper, Bohemian Waxwing, both crossbills (if there is a good cone crop), Evening Grosbeak, and the occasional Three-toed Woodpecker. Pine Siskin can be found at the western end of the Douglas Fir Trail in some winters. Note: The Douglas Fir Trail is closed in winter due to the hazard caused by frozen seepages.

The Bow River Pathway, a paved trail at the base of the escarpment, provides access to an area of riparian woodland. More used by joggers and cyclists (keep well to the side of the path when birding!) than by birders, **Lowery Gardens** has recently gained a reputation as a good alternative to Inglewood Bird Sanctuary for finding migrating passerines in May, August and September. Warblers such as Tennessee, Orange-crowned, Nashville (rare), Yellow, Yellow-rumped, Palm, American Redstart, Connecticut (rare), Mourning (uncommon), MacGillivray's, Common Yellowthroat and Wilson's are generally seen in the carragana shrubs, Red-osier Dogwood and willows along the river's edge. Check the aging poplars away from the paved trail for uncommon species and rarities such as Chestnut-sided, Magnolia, Cape May, Black-throated Green, Blackburnian, Bay-breasted, Black-and–white, and Canada Warblers. Western Tanager and Rose-breasted Grosbeak may also be found here. Breeding species include Downy and Hairy Woodpeckers, Western Wood-Pewee, Gray Catbird and Northern Oriole. A sudden silence may warn of a Merlin or Sharp-shinned Hawk.

A small shallow backwater at the eastern end of Lowery Gardens often has small numbers of ducks and shorebirds. Watch also for Northern Rough-winged and Bank Swallows. The gravel islands in the river provide safe roosting for Canada Goose families. In fall, this stretch of the river is worth checking carefully for a variety of gulls and migrant waterfowl. South of the paved trail and parallel to it, a wide gravel maintenance vehicle path runs past a small swampy area hidden by shrubs, through a field of tall grass containing such varied species as Gray Partridge, Northern Waterthrush, and Clay-colored, Song and Lincoln's Sparrows. In some years Le Conte's Sparrow can also be found here.

The **Quarry Road Trail** is a dirt pathway which extends along the escarpment south of the railway tracks, from the 10 Ave parking lot, parallel to Lowery Gardens, featuring shrubbery and poplars rather than conifers, for most of its one kilometre length. It can be very good for vireos, warblers and sparrows during migration. Gray Catbird, Cedar Waxwing and Clay-colored Sparrow are common near the eastern end. In the late 1980s Rufous-sided Towhee (rarely seen in the city) could be found along this trail. In summer, nesting Red-tailed Hawks and Blue Jays will keep you under surveillance. Access can be gained to Lowery Gardens, across the railway tracks, either half way along the trail or at the western end, making good circular walks from the eastern access points.

A bird checklist for Edworthy Park is available from Natural History Services, Department of Parks/Recreation, The City of Calgary.

ROSS DICKSON

A-4 Bowness Park

Two features make this very popular, urban riverside park of interest to birders: the north-facing escarpment with its dense cover of mature White Spruce and Douglas Fir encourages species diversity; plus the park's location, which helps to intercept migrant passerines moving down the Bow River valley. May, June, August and September are the most rewarding months for birding; it can also be a good winter location. Local rarities recorded here include Black-throated Gray and Bay-breasted Warblers, and Chestnut-backed Chickadee. On busy summer weekends, it is best to plan an early start. For a full day's outing combine Bowness Park with visits to Nose Hill (A-5), the University campus (A-7) or Lowery Gardens (A-3).

Easiest access to the park from most of the city is via the Trans-Canada Highway. From the interchange with Sarcee Trail in northwest Calgary drive 1.3 km west to the Bowfort Road traffic light (Canada Olympic Park is on your left). Turn right and follow the winding road to the stop sign at 85 St NW (signed for Bowness Park). Go left and continue to the 48 Ave NW three-way stop; turn left here and proceed to the park entrance on your right. An alternative route for visitors

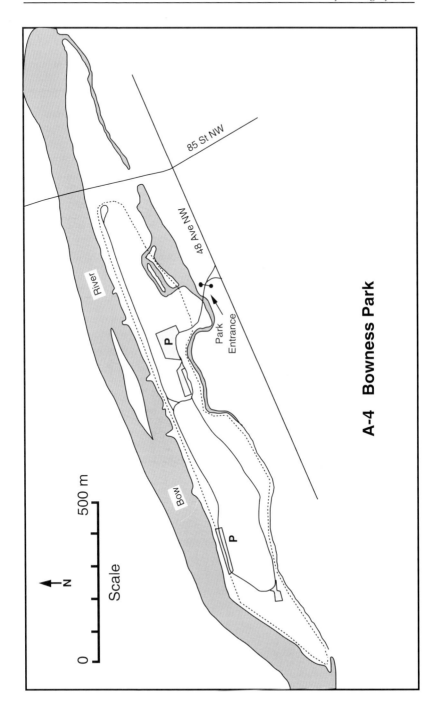

85 St NW

48 Ave NW

River

Park
Entrance

P

Bow

P

500 m

N

Scale

0

A-4 Bowness Park

from the northern part of the city (e.g. Motel Village, sites A-5 and A-7 etc.) is to use westbound Crowchild Trail (turns into Hwy 1A). At Nose Hill Drive turn left (south), head downhill, cross the Bow River and go right at the 48 Ave NW three-way stop to the park (as above).

On your right as you enter the park and cross the backwater channel, is a large lagoon which may have a variety of ducks, Ring-billed Gull and Belted Kingfisher. Straight ahead about 200 m from the entrance is a major parking lot, while following the road another 200 m to the left brings one to a right-hand turn marking the start of the often-congested, 1.6 km long, one-way park loop road.

Bowness Park is best explored on foot, however. Just south of the main parking lot (near the entrance bridge), a red-shale, wheelchair-accessible pathway parallels the narrow backwater channel. At times in fall, the clumps of Red-osier Dogwood, willow and other shrubs by the bridge and flanking the path, can be alive with migrant warblers (particularly Tennessee, Orange-crowned and Wilson's) and sparrows (mostly White-throated and White-crowned with smaller numbers of Song and Lincoln's). In spring, look also for Western Tanager and Rose-breasted Grosbeak. Walking west along this path you should see or hear Black-capped and Boreal Chickadees, Blue Jay, Red-breasted Nuthatch and Golden-crowned Kinglet. Be alert for a Cooper's Hawk or Northern Goshawk (both uncommon) dashing overhead. Great Horned and Northern Saw-whet Owls have also been reported.

From the main parking lot via this path it is about 900 m to the western portion of the island, where a grove of tall conifers interspersed with Aspens dominates the "floodplain". This area consistently provides good birding and should be covered thoroughly. Tucked beneath the spruce-clothed scarp, in late afternoon this area is noticeably cooler and loses its light earlier than most other birding locations within the city. Brown Creeper can be found here throughout the year; in winter this is the most reliable spot in Calgary for finding one. At this season, also look for Three-toed (rare) and Black-backed (very rare) Woodpeckers; flocks of Bohemian Waxwings; Pine Grosbeak; White-winged Crossbill; Common Redpoll; and Pine Siskin (uncommon). From the western tip of the island scan for waterfowl such as Common Merganser and then follow the riverbank path downstream. The rocky shoreline usually hosts Killdeer and Spotted Sandpiper and in fall, small flocks of Pectoral Sandpiper have been noted. Check the outfall across the river for ducks and gulls and watch for the occasional Double-crested Cormorant or Osprey.

If driving the loop, stop in the lot located 0.9 km from the park entrance. Walk southwest from this lot for 150 m (parallel to the road) along an embankment (which can provide excellent, less neck-stretching views of tree-top warblers) to join the red shale path.

Downstream (east) of the amusement rides area, beyond the 85 St bridge, is a 750 m stretch of Balsam Poplar woodland with an under-story of wild rose, River Birch and dogwood. This is worth checking during the migration periods and in summer when the bulk of the park is overrun with people.

The washrooms near the lagoon are open year-round. Snacks are available from the adjacent pavilion in summer.

RICHARD THOMAS

A-5 Nose Hill Park

Nose Hill Park is part of a broad prairie plateau located in the north-west corner of Calgary and which is visible from some distance away. It is comprised primarily of mixed grassland, with numerous ravines radiating outward from the central plateau. There are Aspen groves and dense shrubby thickets as well as two abandoned gravel pits. Access is relatively easy. On the eastern side there are parking areas off 14 St NW at 64 Ave and Berkley Gate. The parking area on the western side is located at the intersection of Shaganappi Trail and Edgemont Blvd. To enter the park on the south side, park just off John Laurie Blvd in the vicinity of Brisebois Drive, Charleswood Drive or 19 St NW. In this case it will be necessary to cross John Laurie Blvd on foot.

From a birder's point of view, an outstanding feature of Nose Hill is the fact that it is the only location within the city where Sharp-tailed Grouse may be found. A small population has inhabited this grass-land for a number of years. The grouse may be encountered almost

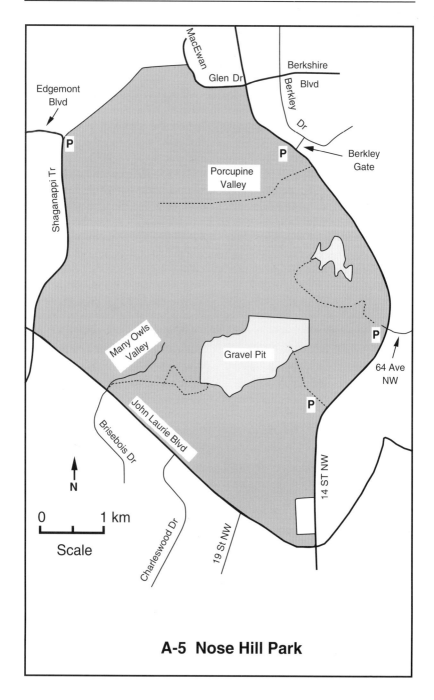

A-5 Nose Hill Park

anywhere on the hill. Unfortunately, dogs are still allowed to roam loose in the park, putting ground-dwelling species under great stress. Birders should use care when looking for the grouse, to avoid compounding the problem.

The unique habitat of Nose Hill has attracted other uncommon species such as Long-eared Owl, Rock Wren and Lazuli Bunting. Although Long-eared Owls are reported very infrequently around Calgary, they have nested on Nose Hill in recent years. The groves and thickets in Many Owls and Porcupine valleys are the best places to look for owls; early morning or late evening are the best times. Historically, the large gravel pit on Nose Hill has been the only area within the city where Rock Wren has been recorded with any regularity. The last report, however, was of an adult and four juveniles in 1987. It may be that attempts to tidy up the gravel pit have changed the habitat too much for this species. Lazuli Bunting nested on Nose Hill in 1985 and 1986, with singing males being most readily observed in the dense shrub patches on the southern slope between Brisebois and Charleswood.

In summer, listen for the trill of Baird's Sparrow amongst the grasses of the plateau, although it is more numerous in some years than others and may not be present. Sprague's Pipit can be heard singing in this area too. Nose Hill's prairie habitat has proved attractive not only to Baird's, but to 13 other species of sparrow as well. It is an extremely accessible area for finding native grassland species such as Clay-colored, Vesper and Savannah Sparrows, with Lincoln's possible in damper areas. Listen for Le Conte's Sparrow in the damper areas too, but it can also be found in dry grassland.

You should encounter Gray Partridge, Horned Lark, Western Meadow-lark, Brewer's Blackbird and possibly, Ring-necked Pheasant. Both Swainson's and Red-tailed Hawks can be seen hunting the abundant rodent life here. Watch too for American Kestrel hovering above potential prey. If you are lucky, you may see both Merlin and Prairie Falcon as well. In the thickets, watch for Alder Flycatcher (occasionally in Porcupine Valley), Gray Catbird, Brown Thrasher and American Goldfinch.

Nose Hill is a productive winter birding location for certain species, particularly raptors. Rough-legged Hawk, Merlin and Prairie Falcon are recorded here regularly, with Northern Goshawk, Gyrfalcon,

Short-eared Owl and Northern Shrike seen occasionally as well. Snow Buntings may be found on the windswept grasslands of the plateau, particularly near the large gravel pit.

On November 22, 1989 a Northern Wheatear was photographed on Nose Hill, the first documented record for Alberta.

TERRY KOROLYK

A-6 Glenmore Reservoir and The Weaselhead Natural Area

Glenmore Reservoir, the city of Calgary's major water supply, was created in 1933 with completion of the dam across the Elbow River valley. Today, this deep waterbody covers 429 hectares and at certain times of the year it can provide some of the city's finest birding. Large tracts of the valley surrounding the Reservoir have been preserved as a public park; here the main areas of interest to birders are the Weaselhead Natural Area at the western end, and the South Glenmore Natural Area.

Access to Glenmore Park and the Reservoir from the north is either from the southern end of Crowchild Trail, or from 37 St SW and 66 Ave. The southern shore is reached from 90 Ave SW and 24 St, or from 90 Ave and Oakmount Drive.

The best months for birding the Reservoir are April and the first two weeks of May, and October-November. A telescope is a must at these times as the rafts of waterfowl tend to stay well out from the shore. More than 15 km of trails may be walked around the Reservoir but usually the most productive viewing is from near the Canoe and Rowing Club on the north side, and the Sailing School on the south, near the 90 Ave and 24 St car park.

Glare and wind conditions can make birding difficult at Glenmore. Light conditions on the north shore are best early in the morning; viewing from the canoe club is best after the sun has been "up" a few

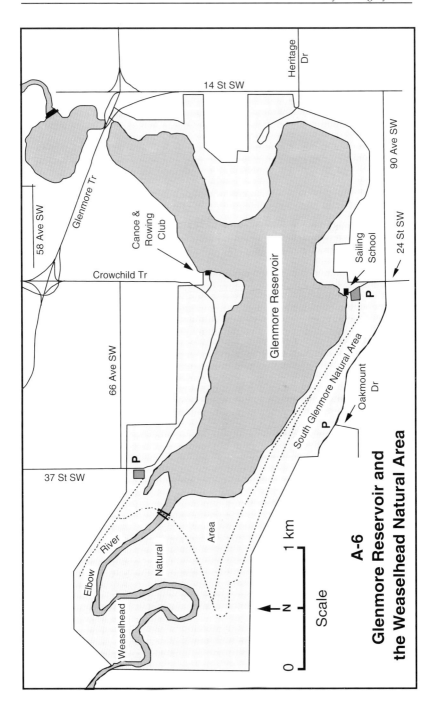

A-6
**Glenmore Reservoir and
the Weaselhead Natural Area**

hours (so you're not looking into the glare); the west end is best in the morning; and on the south side, light conditions are best during late morning and the afternoon. The canoe club area is sheltered from westerly winds; it has deeper water and freezes later, so it can be attractive to loons, Oldsquaw and diving ducks later in the season. Loons can occur anywhere, however, even in the shallows at the western end.

In spring, the first area to become ice-free is at the western end where the Elbow River enters the Reservoir; check here for early arrivals. In fall, freeze-up can be quite late, allowing the build-up of large concentrations of waterfowl; at the western end the numbers of swans, geese and gulls can provide quite a spectacle at times. Uncommon species and migrants to watch for include: both Tundra and Trumpeter Swans; Greater Scaup (fall); Oldsquaw (Oct-Nov); Surf Scoter (April-May, Oct); White-winged Scoter (late April-May, Oct-Nov); Hooded Merganser (mid-April and May, Sept-Nov); and Red-breasted Merganser (April, Oct-Nov). Black Scoter has been recorded in fall on several occasions but identification requires care. Late fall is the time to look for loons: Pacific is seen most years; Red-throated is rare. In 1979, a Yellow-billed Loon remained on the Reservoir from November 4 to 11. Perhaps the most bizarre species to have been recorded at Glenmore to date was an Ancient Murrelet, photographed here on October 17, 1982.

Just prior to freeze-up it can also be worthwhile checking the smaller waterbody NORTH of Glenmore Trail (park at Lakeview Golf Club— 19 St and 58 Ave SW). This occasionally holds the last loons, grebes and diving ducks such as scoters.

The **Weaselhead Natural Area** encompasses the valley and final major meander of the Elbow River before it enters the Reservoir, and the delta environment that the river continues to build. The vegetation ranges from emergent aquatic plants through willows, Aspen and Balsam Poplar to mature White Spruce forest. May and June are the most rewarding months for birding here.

The access trail to the Weaselhead on the northern side of the Reservoir begins at the 37 St parking area. The disturbed grassland to the west often has such typical species as Clay-colored, Vesper and Savannah Sparrows and Western Meadowlark. Grasshopper Sparrow has been found here occasionally but should not be expected. In summer, the trail down the escarpment may yield Rufous Hummingbird,

Yellow-bellied Sapsucker, House Wren, Gray Catbird, Brown Thrasher, Cedar Waxwing, Yellow Warbler, Rufous-sided Towhee, and (sometimes) Purple Finch. Birds to watch for in the mature Balsam Poplar forest at the base of the escarpment include Northern Flicker, Western Wood-Pewee, Least Flycatcher and Northern Oriole. An area of dense willow surrounds the first footbridge. Watch and listen here for both Alder and Willow Flycatchers, Veery, Northern Waterthrush, Common Yellowthroat, and various species of swallow. A male Kentucky Warbler (Alberta's first) was photographed here on June 18, 1988. Check the river also; you may see Common Goldeneye, Spotted Sandpiper and Belted Kingfisher. After crossing the footbridge head west along a dirt trail. Birds to watch for in this area include Ruffed Grouse, Mourning Dove, Great Horned Owl, Olive-sided Flycatcher, Eastern Phoebe, Black-capped Chickadee, Red-breasted Nuthatch, Brown Creeper and Purple Finch. In the burned area watch for Three-toed Woodpecker.

The trail along the north side of the river, west from the 37 St parking area leads eventually to the top of a high cliff above the river. This is the most reliable spot in the city for Rufous Hummingbird. Several males usually guard territories here from late May to mid-July. Just past this point the trail turns south and reaches a small beaver pond inside the major loop of the Elbow River. This area is good for Northern Waterthrush and Purple Finch. The trail is subject to horse traffic and can become very cut-up and muddy. Boots should be worn and care taken on the steeper sections.

On the southern side, in the **South Glenmore Natural Area,** a strip of shrubbery extending along the embankment for one kilometre west of the car park at 90 Ave and 24 St can be very good for migrant warblers in spring and fall. West of this, near the parking area at 90 Ave and Oakmount Drive, is a stand of mature White Spruce which can produce Ruffed Grouse, Three-toed Woodpecker, Boreal Chickadee, Pine Grosbeak, both Red and White-winged Crossbills (erratic, especially Red) and Pine Siskin. From here, check the mudflats for waterfowl and shorebirds. Further west, trails above and below the escarpment link up with the Weaselhead Natural Area. Ruby-throated Hummingbird can be found in the swampy open glades along the bottom of the escarpment, and Sora and Le Conte's Sparrow in the marshy area, known as the "beaverpond", at the western end where the bike pathway turns north. By following the bike pathway, the footbridge across the Elbow River can be reached. It is approximately 5 km one way from the 24 St parking area to the bridge. Trails to the west can be followed to reach the riverbank and several areas of White Spruce.

In October and November, both the north and south (by the 24 St corrals) shores should be checked for late Mountain Bluebirds and Northern Shrikes. The "cliffs" on the northern shore are sometimes good for raptor watching in fall and winter. Species to watch for include: accipiters (especially Northern Goshawk), buteos, Gyrfalcon and Merlin.

Glenmore Park is intensively used for recreational purposes; the natural areas are best birded early in the morning. Washrooms are available year-round in the vicinity of the parking areas.

DAVE ELPHINSTONE and ANDREW SLATER

A-7 The University of Calgary Campus

Located in northwest Calgary, the 122 ha university campus was recently described in a popular student guide as one of the nation's most boring. Fortunately for birders the outlook is more encouraging. Use of public transport to reach the U. of C. is recommended (for Transit Information call 276–7801). If driving from downtown Calgary take Crowchild Trail (north) and University Drive. Parking on campus can be frustrating, especially just before 1:00 and 7:00 p.m. Only on Sundays is most parking free. Just north of the arch marking the main (University Drive) entrance is an information booth where visitors can obtain a campus map.

The most productive season in terms of species diversity and abundance is fall when, during favourable migration conditions, almost anything can show up—with the passage of warblers, sparrows and other passerines being especially noteworthy. The next most productive is spring migration, followed by summer and finally, winter. Glance up occasionally as both eagle species, accipiters, various buteos and Osprey have been observed over-flying the campus.

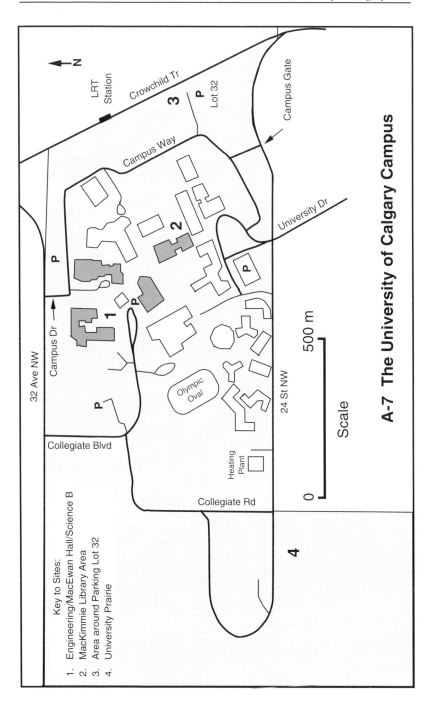

Key to Sites:
1. Engineering/MacEwan Hall/Science B
2. MacKimmie Library Area
3. Area around Parking Lot 32
4. University Prairie

Scale

0   500 m

A-7 The University of Calgary Campus

The four most consistently-productive birding spots on campus are described as a walking tour. To bird all these sites thoroughly takes half a day although the 4 km-long route can be completed in as little as 1 1/2 hours. Visitors with limited time are recommended to try either sites 1 and 2 (all year), sites 2 and 3 (fall), or site 4 (all year). Birding the U. of C. can be combined with a visit to nearby Nose Hill (A-5) or Lowery Gardens (A-3).

1. Engineering/MacEwan Hall/Science B
This area is located south of the northeast (Campus Drive) entrance to campus from 32 Ave NW. The large stands of conifers along the east side of Engineering Blocks A and B and around the Globe Cairn on the west side of these blocks are one of the better sites in Calgary for cross-bills in fall and winter when the cone crop is good. These birds can be surprisingly hard to see: watch for falling cones and cone-scales; listen for their distinctive calls and sounds accompanying cone dismember-ment. Generally, White-wingeds are the more common and occur in larger flocks (up to 40 birds) than Red Crossbills (average flock size 4–8 birds). Check the shrubs for warblers during fall migration.

From Engineering continue south to the area between MacEwan Hall and Science B. At times this locality can be a real hot spot for birds. During spring and fall the lawns hereabouts host Ring-billed Gulls. In winter flocks of Bohemian Waxwings may frequent the poplars around MacEwan Hall. The mixed stand of trees 40 m southwest of the main Science B entrance always merits careful attention. In fall, the cone-bearing birches attract flocks of Common Redpoll, Pine Siskin and, occasionally, several warbler species and Red-breasted Nuthatch. During fall check the bushes around Science A and B for migrating sparrows; White-throated and White-crowned being the common species. Continue south past the Swann Mall hillock (with its large metal "Prairie Chicken" sculpture) along the east side of the Library.

2. MacKimmie Library Area
During fall migration the trees and shrubs bordering the east side of the Library and between it and the Administration building, can be excellent for both warblers and sparrows. Warblers, in approximate decreasing order of abundance, include: Yellow-rumped (mostly "Myrtles"), Wilson's, Yellow, Orange-crowned and Tennessee, with additional species (e.g. Northern Waterthrush) possible but not to be expected. In September, small numbers of Blackpoll Warblers appear

annually in this area. The shrubbery may host Chipping, Clay-
colored, Savannah, Lincoln's, White-throated and White-crowned
Sparrows. Fox Sparrow has been recorded. In late afternoon/early
evening the small pond 50 m northeast of the Library entrance sometimes attracts good numbers of bathing birds.

Continue past the Education tower towards the southeast corner of
campus located between Crowchild Trail and 24 Ave NW. En route,
watch and listen for Merlins with their distinctive "charging" flight
and staccato "kee-kee–kee" calls. Both Merlins and Prairie Falcons
perch on several of the taller buildings on campus. In recent years,
favoured sites have included Earth Sciences, Biosciences, Social
Science, the Education and Library towers, and the T.V. antenna atop
Kananaskis Hall. Bear in mind these falcons often choose a ledge
some way below the top of the building.

3. Area around Parking Lot 32
This area of mixed deciduous and coniferous trees and shrubs lies east
of the southeast entrance to the U. of C. (Campus Gate). It comes into
its own during fall migration when almost any regular Calgary
migrant passerine can show up here including most of the warbler
and sparrow species listed above, plus Western Tanager and Rose-
breasted Grosbeak. MacGillivray's Warbler has been seen here.

From Campus Gate proceed west along 24 Ave NW for about 300 m to
the main (south) campus entrance on University Drive. Merlins have
nested in the stand of spruce just east of the Arch. Continue west
along 24 Ave past the Heating Plant; watch for Bohemian Waxwings,
Pine Grosbeaks and crossbills here in winter.

4. University Prairie
At the nearby junction of Collegiate Road with 24 Ave, cross the latter
and proceed 30 m south from the fire hydrant to the northeast corner
of University Prairie. This expanse of semi-natural grassland also contains scattered trees and scrub. Enter via the gap in the fence, turn
right and walk along the fence for about 75 m to where the path forks.
Aim southwest, i.e. towards the tallest transmitter mast on the hill
across the Bow River valley. Bushes near this fork host breeding Clay-
colored Sparrows; Savannah (and perhaps Vesper) Sparrows may also
nest on the Prairie. Lincoln's, White-throated and White-crowned
Sparrows can be found on passage and Le Conte's is a remote

possibility. Mountain Bluebird and Townsend's Solitaire (fall) may occur during migration. Snow Buntings sometimes pass through in hard winter weather and in fall and winter, a Northern Shrike may linger for a day or two. In summer, Swainson's and Red-tailed Hawks and American Kestrel hunt over the Prairie and breed nearby. Coveys of Gray Partridge may be encountered anywhere in this area.

From the NE entrance, following the fence west and then north brings one to the "Biology Plot". Northern Goshawk has occurred here in winter. In fall, the trees in the northwest corner (together with the Quaking Aspen grove north of the Olympic Oval) host a spectacular roost of up to 3,000 American Crows. Numbers start to build during late summer and peak in Sept-Oct. During mild years small numbers of crows may overwinter. University Prairie should be avoided at lunchtime when it is overrun with hordes of joggers, dog-walkers and mountain bikers. Warning: visitors should take great care to avoid the innumerable Richardson's Ground Squirrel burrows that riddle the grassland and paths.

Birding the U. of C. campus offers an experience unlike any other locality described in this book. It can be a crowded environment and birders are advised to avoid the lunch hour (12:00–1:00 p.m.) and the 10-minute period before each hour (when classes change). One must be prepared for stares, questions and comments—definitely not the place for birders too shy to do their "psshing" in public! On the plus side, the U. of C. is much quieter than other popular Calgary birding spots on weekends, holidays and during the summer months. Most buildings have readily-accessible washrooms. Food and drink are available in MacEwan Hall (ground floor) and at the "food fair" on the main floor of the MacEwan Student Centre.

RICHARD THOMAS

A-8 Winter Birding
Along The Bow River

Due to warmer winters and water from storm sewers and other sources entering the river within the city, the Bow now remains partially open throughout the winter from the Inglewood Bird Sanctuary downstream, and mostly open south of the Bonnybrook Sewage Treatment Plant. This open water is utilized by huge numbers of Mallards, with over 10,000 being usually recorded on the Calgary Christmas Bird Count. Good numbers of Canada Goose (about 200) and Common Goldeneye (up to 1,500) also over-winter, while Green-winged Teal, Northern Pintail, Gadwall, American Wigeon, Lesser Scaup, Barrow's Goldeneye, Bufflehead and Common Merganser occur in small numbers. Redhead, Harlequin Duck and Hooded Merganser can usually be found on an annual basis. Canvasback and Ring-necked Duck are possibilities.

Almost any kind of waterbird may turn up, especially in November and December, when according to the field guides they should be on the west coast or much farther south. Notable occurrences of wintering individuals in recent years have included Double-crested Cormorant, Black-crowned Night-Heron, Tundra Swan, Trumpeter Swan and Oldsquaw. The large quantity of potential prey attracts several raptor species, especially Bald Eagle and Rough-legged Hawk, but also including the occasional Cooper's Hawk, Northern Goshawk, Red-tailed Hawk, Gyrfalcon and Prairie Falcon. The raptors tend to be most numerous in November, December and March. Inglewood, Carburn Park and the Forest Lawn stormwater retention pond (see route B-5), are the locations in Calgary where Gyrfalcons have been most frequently reported in recent winters. Merlin is a year-round resident and may be seen anywhere along the river. While some birds may be found wherever open water exists, good concentrations occur at certain locations. These will be described from north to south.

Inglewood Bird Sanctuary (See site A-1)
This section of the river can be a hot spot in November and early December, with good numbers of waterbirds remaining while conditions are favourable. As the Sanctuary is located upstream from the sewage treatment plant the river mostly freezes over during the

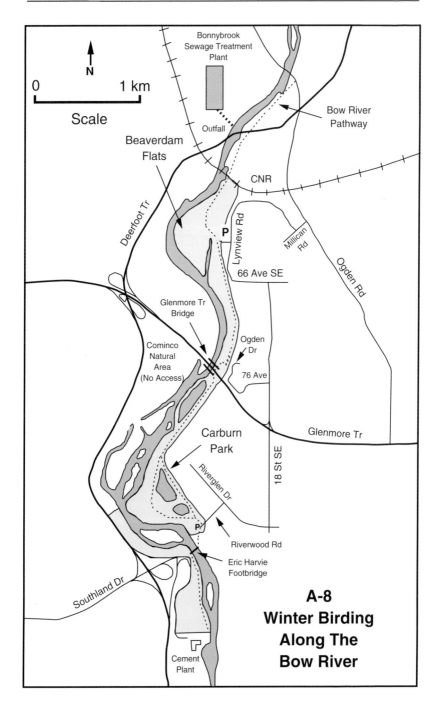

N

0   1 km

Scale

Bonnybrook
Sewage Treatment
Plant

Bow River
Pathway

Outfall

Beaverdam
Flats

CNR

Deerfoot Tr

P

Lynview Rd

Millican Rd

66 Ave SE

Ogden Rd

Glenmore Tr
Bridge

Ogden
Dr

Cominco
Natural
Area
(No Access)

76 Ave

Carburn
Park

Glenmore Tr

Riverglen Dr

18 St SE

P

Riverwood Rd

Eric Harvie
Footbridge

Southland Dr

Cement
Plant

**A-8
Winter Birding
Along The
Bow River**

depths of winter. Species to watch for at Inglewood in winter include Gyrfalcon, Common Snipe, Northern Saw-whet Owl, Belted Kingfisher and Northern Flicker.

An alternative access point for viewing the river at Inglewood is from the Inglewood Golf and Curling Club. This is reached by taking the Peigan Trail exit from the Deerfoot Trail, turning left (north) onto 25 St SE and driving 0.9 km to Gosling Way. Park in the parking lot and walk along the paved service road beside the clubhouse to the river.

Beaverdam Flats Natural Area
From the Glenmore Trail head north on 18 St SE, then left at the T-intersection with 66 Ave. Continue west to the escarpment, where the road then turns north and becomes Lynnview Road. The parking area and river access is on the left, opposite Lynnview Way. This is marked by a Bow River Pathway sign. From the parking area follow the paved trail down the escarpment, through the woodland to the southern tip of the flats. This woodland is not as productive as Carburn Park in winter. The species most often seen include Downy Woodpecker, Black-capped Chickadee, White-breasted Nuthatch, Bohemian Waxwing and Common Redpoll. Check the chickadee flocks for the occasional Brown Creeper. Gray Partridge, Ring-necked Pheasant and Great Horned Owl occur here too but are more likely to be encountered as you walk north along the riverbank.

The stretch of river from the southern end of Beaverdam Flats north to the Bonnybrook Sewage Treatment Plant can be most rewarding. Rather than following the paved trail north through the woods look for the system of minor trails along the river's edge. Common Goldeneye are abundant and these should be checked for the occasional Bufflehead. Towards the northern end of the flats watch for a small lagoon set into the opposite bank. This is probably the most reliable place within the city for Green-winged Teal in winter; Northern Pintail is regular here too. Check the tree stumps around the lagoon—a Great Blue Heron sometimes roosts here. As you proceed north check the ducks tucked in under the opposite bank or around any storm sewer outfall. Gadwall, American Wigeon, Lesser Scaup and Common Merganser can usually be found here. Watch for Harlequin Duck in the rough water in the vicinity of the railway and Deerfoot Trail bridges. At least one Bald Eagle should be seen; Killdeer and Rusty Blackbird are possible.

Glenmore Trail Bridge

From the Glenmore Trail turn north on 18 St SE and then left on 76 Ave at the first lights. Continue to the escarpment and park along Ogden Drive, close to the Bow River Pathway sign. Follow the paved trail down to the bridge. The fast flowing water around the gravel bars on both sides of the bridge is the most reliable location in the city for Harlequin Duck. From the bridge walk north along the unpaved trail at the water's edge to the sweeping bend. A large raft of ducks concentrates at this bend; Gadwall, Redhead, Lesser Scaup, Bufflehead and Hooded Merganser might be found here. The paved trail can be followed south from the Glenmore Trail bridge for access to the northern part of the Carburn Park area.

Carburn Park

Carburn Park is reached by turning south from Glenmore Trail onto 18 St SE, right onto Riverglen Drive and then left onto Riverwood Road. From the parking lot walk along the paved trail around the north side of the lagoon to the river. This spot is opposite the Cominco Natural Area, a privately-owned property containing run-off channels from a fertilizer plant that introduce enriched warm water to the river. Until recently, the canals have been almost choked with birds in winter but since 1990 less warm water has been discharged into them and should the plant close, as is expected, then these canals are unlikely to remain open during the coldest months. As there is no public access to the Cominco area, a spotting scope is very useful for viewing the canals. Great Blue Herons sometimes spend part of the winter on the Cominco property and may be seen from here. A Red-tailed (Harlan's ssp.) Hawk has frequented the woods at Cominco for several winters. Follow the riverbank southward from the Cominco area. The river curves to the left after about 300 m to a stretch where it runs almost due east between tall trees on both banks. Bald Eagles often perch in these trees. From the eastern end of this stretch a short walk through the woods will bring you back to the parking lot.

To access the western bank, walk south from the parking lot along the paved trail and cross the river on the Eric Harvie footbridge. The stretch of river immediately south of the footbridge is favoured by Canada Goose and Barrow's Goldeneye. The paved trail can be followed for about 0.5 km south as far as the cement plant. Great Horned Owls are sometimes found in the small wooded section. The footpath on the western side of the river north from the footbridge should also be followed along the edge of a shallow river overflow channel; Green-winged Teal, Killdeer and Common Snipe are possible here. Road access to this stretch of the western riverbank is possible from the eastern end of Southland Drive, at the lowest (east) end of the ramp onto northbound Deerfoot Trail. Other birds that may be seen in the Carburn Park area include Merlin, Gray Partridge, Ring-necked Pheasant, Belted Kingfisher, Downy Woodpecker, Northern Flicker, White-breasted Nuthatch, American Tree Sparrow, Rusty Blackbird and Common Redpoll.

Fish Creek Provincial Park (See site A-2)
The Bow River flows through Fish Creek Park for a distance of nearly 4 km, most of which remains unfrozen throughout the winter. While the density of birds here is not usually as great as at Carburn Park, good numbers can nearly always be found and several rarities have occurred.

The most northerly access is at Mallard Point which is at the eastern end of Canyon Meadows Drive. From Mallard Point the riverbank follows the shore of Poplar Island for about 2 km south, there are no established trails and bush-whacking is fairly tough. There are several other access points off Bow Bottom Trail which are all linked by a paved trail and walking the riverbank between them is considerably easier. Follow Bow Bottom Trail south past Sikome Lake to the road terminus at a parking area just south of the Marquis of Lorne Trail (Hwy 22X) bridge. From this point the riverbank can be hiked further south to beyond the city limits. Two Oldsquaw wintered in this area in 1990. Bald Eagles are most often observed along the stretch just north of the Hwy 22X bridge.

ANDREW SLATER and JOAN McDONALD

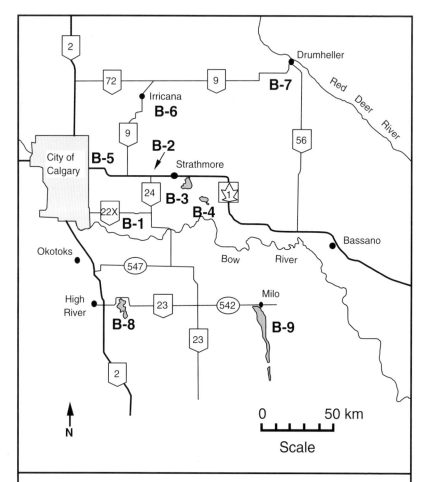

Section B: The Prairies

B-1 Shepard Sloughs, Dalemead Reservoir and
      Wyndham-Carseland Provincial Park
B-2 Sadler's Slough
B-3 Eagle Lake
B-4 Namaka Lake
B-5 McElroy Slough Driving Route
B-6 The Irricana Area and Bruce Lake Driving Route
B-7 The Drumheller Area
B-8 Frank Lake
B-9 McGregor Lake

B-1 Shepard Sloughs,
Dalemead Reservoir and
Wyndham-Carseland Provincial Park

This route is most rewarding during the migration months (late March to early June and from mid-July to late October) when large numbers of waterfowl and shorebirds should be found, together with good numbers of raptors. At least five hours are needed to cover the 120 km roundtrip to Johnson's Island. During the peak fall migration period, Dalemead Reservoir and the Carseland Weir area may each require that amount of time to bird thoroughly.

Directions are given from the junction of Glenmore Trail (Secondary Road [S.R.] 560) and 52 St SE, i.e. the last stop sign on Glenmore Trail inside the city. Take an odometer reading here, then continue east for 3.2 km and turn right (south) on Shepard Road. Immediately after passing the village hall in **Shepard**, turn left at the intersection with 114 Ave and drive east for about 2 km. In spring and early summer a large wet pasture on the south side of the road may be good for shorebirds and puddle ducks. In 1989, the first nesting record in the Calgary Region for Black-necked Stilt occurred here, with three young being fledged. On the north side of the road (west of the shallow slough area), within the Richardson's Ground Squirrel colony, Burrowing Owls nested for several years in the early 1980s.

Turn round at the first farm driveway, return to the intersection in Shepard and head south. The fields on either side may have dry-land shorebirds such as Lesser Golden-Plover and Long-billed Curlew. Burrowing Owls have nested in the grassy pastures along this stretch—again, study the ground squirrel colonies. Short-eared Owls and, in winter, Snowy Owls are frequently found in this vicinity.

Immediately after the bend in the road, a shallow slough on the right contains water in wet summers and is an alkali bowl at other times. In August 1986 a Rufous-necked Stint was observed here, together with many other shorebirds. One kilometre further south is the junction with Hwy 22X (162 Ave SE). Listen for Sora in the small sloughs at this corner.

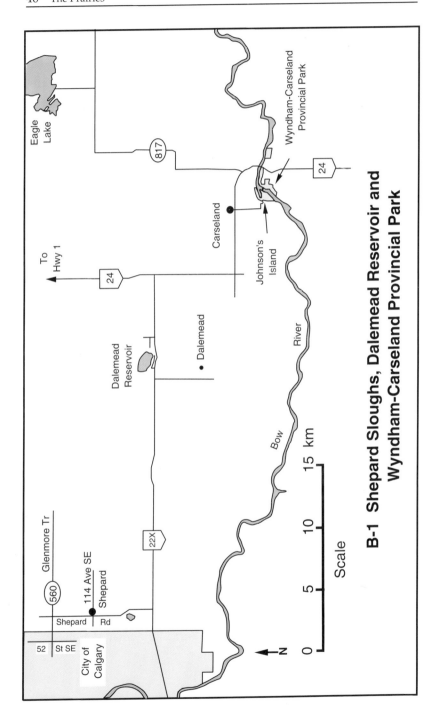

B-1 Shepard Sloughs, Dalemead Reservoir and Wyndham-Carseland Provincial Park

Check your odometer here, turn left and drive east on Hwy 22X for
18 km, to the junction with an unnumbered road to the right marked
"Dalemead". Ahead of you the road begins a gentle curve. Slow
down and watch for a dirt track on the left, 0.8 km past the Dalemead
junction. Although there are no signs posted, this is the access to the
southwestern corner of **Dalemead Reservoir** (also known as Weed
Lake). Turn left here and then right, parallel to the fence. If the track
looks at all muddy, PARK HERE AND WALK, as it has mired several
unwary birders' vehicles. If the track is dry, it can be safely, but slowly,
driven for 0.6 km to a stile through the fence marked with a "No Pro-
pellers" sign, which presumably means that powerboats are prohibit-
ed. Lighting conditions are best here in the afternoon.

Dalemead Reservoir is a large irrigation storage reservoir that is usually full of water in spring and early summer, but has a reduced level in
late summer and fall. Consequently, there is an abundance of waterfowl present during spring migration, but usually few shorebirds.
During fall migration however, large numbers of many species are
present. In recent years this has been probably the best location for fall
shorebirds in the Calgary Region. Rarities reported have included
Spotted Redshank (1987), Wandering Tattler (1988), Ruff and Sharp-
tailed Sandpiper (both 1990). The area most commonly birded is the
southern one third of the shoreline, as the easiest access points are at
the southeastern and southwestern corners. However, if sufficient
time is available it would probably be worthwhile walking north
along the eastern and western shorelines. There is virtually no cover
present—the whole area behind the shoreline consisting of rough
grassland and weedy areas, with cultivated fields beyond. Upland
Sandpiper has been seen in the weedy areas in late May and Chestnut-
collared Longspur in summer.

To reach the southeastern access point from the stile, return to the
highway, turn left and continue 2.6 km east past the power lines, to the
first road heading north. Turn left here then, immediately before the
bridge over the irrigation canal, turn left again onto a narrow dirt road
(only if the road surface is bare and dry) along the south side of the
canal to a parking area and another stile. It is necessary to walk for a
short distance along the canal bank (this can be good for shorebirds
when the water level is low) to reach the reservoir embankment. The
light is best at this access point early in the morning.

Retrace your route back to Hwy 22X, turn left and continue eastward to the T-intersection with Hwy 24. Turn right (south), then left at the 4-way stop with a red flashing light, following Hwy 24. The village of Carseland with its grain elevators is now visible ahead on the left. Opposite the access road to the village, turn right onto a gravel road marked **Johnson's Island (Carseland Weir)**. This road is the entrance to a reliable migrant trap for waterfowl, shorebirds and passerines. About 2.3 km south of the highway, the gravel road turns sharply left through a Texas gate and proceeds 0.8 km eastward along the edge of the escarpment, with spectacular views of the Bow River valley. Then it makes a hairpin turn to the right and descends to the valley bottom by means of switchbacks. At the bottom of the hill, follow the right fork to the parking area by the river's edge. This 7 km roundtrip from the highway is not recommended after a heavy rain or snowfall, when the switchback portion may not be passable by automobiles.

The reservoir formed in the Bow River by the weir is one of the first places in the Calgary Region to become ice-free in spring, and usually has a good assortment of waterfowl present before the end of March. In the past few years, a flock of over 100 American White Pelicans has been present above the weir from late July to October. The spectacle of these huge birds as they soar majestically above the valley, or fish in unison in the river, is alone worth the drive from Calgary.

North of the parking area, along the bottom of the escarpment, is a backwater channel. The mudflats here can be very productive for shorebirds in both spring and fall. The trail which heads east along the shore of the backwater reaches the river downstream of the weir; the gravel bars here are used for resting by several species of gulls, ducks and Canada Geese. Between the gravel bars and the shore are more mudflats. This is the best location in the immediate vicinity for shorebirds. The trail may be followed southward along the river's edge to the weir and along the top of the levee back to your vehicle.

If time is short, you can retrace your route up the escarpment back to Hwy 24 where you turn left for the return to Calgary. The quickest route is via Hwy 22X to Hwy 2. An alternative route to north Calgary would be to continue north on Hwy 24 to the Trans-Canada Highway (Hwy 1). This intersection is the location of Sadler's Slough (see site B-2).

If time permits during late August, warbler watching is usually better on the south side of the Bow River than at Johnson's Island. From Carseland, turn right (east) onto Hwy 24 and continue past S.R. 817 (a connector route to Eagle Lake, see site B-3), cross over the bridge and watch for the entrance to Wyndham-Carseland Provincial Park on the right hand side of the road (5 km). The access road forks immediately, with the left fork leading through open farmland to a parking area at the south end of the weir; good views of waterbirds can be obtained from here.

The right fork enters the park (day use free), and turns left immediately on entering the campground. This is situated in a large tract of riparian woodland. The road continues westward for about 2 km through the campground before emerging into a parking and picnic area by the river, opposite the gravel bars. A wide variety of warblers and other small woodland birds may be seen from the riverbank trail, which passes through abundant dogwood and willow shrubbery. Watch for raptors along the escarpment at any season. Upstream towards the weir, the trail passes through a lawn area with scattered bushes—this can be rewarding for sparrows.

There are pit toilets at the picnic area and throughout the campground. Gas and food are available in Carseland.

Caution: During the fall waterfowl hunting season, which runs from mid-September to early December, locations such as Dalemead Reservoir, Carseland Weir, Eagle, Namaka and McGregor lakes, and the Brooks area can be heavily shot over. Birding during this period will be more enjoyable if you restrict your visits to Sundays, when shooting is not permitted.

ANDREW SLATER

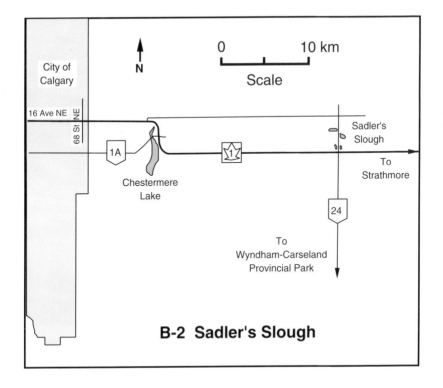

B-2 Sadler's Slough

Sadler's Slough is a series of small, interconnected sloughs and creeks (part of a Ducks Unlimited wetland habitat conservation project) stretching for about two kilometres along a gravel road, 10 km west of Strathmore. It is an excellent location for observing the spring shore-bird migration. To reach Sadler's Slough, drive east on the Trans-Canada Highway for 30 km from the traffic light at 16 Ave and 68 St NE in Calgary and watch for the sign on the right indicating Hwy 24 to Vulcan and Lethbridge. TURN LEFT at this intersection onto the unnumbered gravel road heading north.

From late April to early June, the whole two kilometres from the Trans-Canada north to the first farm should be driven slowly, observing carefully on both sides. Because the habitat is so close to the road, much of it no more than 50 metres away, this location offers an out-standing opportunity for viewing many kinds of shorebirds and surface-feeding ducks at very close range. This is extremely useful for comparing the different kinds of peeps and other small shorebirds together. A telescope on a window-mount is a great help for viewing the birds closely without disturbing them.

The three common peeps of the Calgary Region (Semipalmated, Least and Baird's Sandpipers) are usually present during this period, often in good numbers. Western and White-rumped Sandpipers turn up in very small numbers from time to time. Other migrant shorebirds which may be expected are: Black-bellied and Semipalmated Plovers; Greater and Lesser Yellowlegs; Solitary Sandpiper; Sanderling; Pectoral and Stilt Sandpipers; and both dowitchers. More unusual species such as Hudsonian Godwit and Dunlin might occur. In the second half of May, Lesser Golden-Plover should be watched for in the plowed fields immediately beyond the wetlands.

Together with these shorebirds will be several species of surface-feeding ducks, including Cinnamon Teal, and possibly five species of Grebe: Pied-billed, Horned, Red-necked, Eared and Western. The most northerly slough on the right hand side is larger than the others and may contain Double-crested Cormorant, some diving ducks and, in the second half of May, Red-necked Phalarope. At this time too, there may be the occasional Greater White-fronted Goose among the numerous Canadas.

By the time the fall shorebird migration gets underway in earnest, around the middle of July, only the larger sloughs usually contain water and most of the muddy edges will have dried up. At this time the productive habitat is restricted to the two small sloughs by the Trans-Canada Highway and the two larger ones at the northern end of the complex. The location is still worth visiting however, as any of the migrants may turn up again, though in smaller numbers. Late July is a good time to look for the occasional Short-billed Dowitcher, as this species usually passes through before most of the more numerous Long-billeds arrive.

Sadler's Slough is only 15 to 20 minutes driving time from the city lim-its and may require from half an hour to two hours to bird thoroughly. The visibility is good for most of the day, though very early morning

and late evening should be avoided if possible. By driving north to
the first intersection and turning left (3.2 km from the Trans-Canada),
an alternative route back to Calgary on a gravel road may be taken.
This goes through farmland and past several interesting small sloughs
and McElroy Slough (B-5) before rejoining the Trans-Canada Highway.
Sadler's Slough can also be visited in combination with other locations
in the vicinity such as Eagle Lake (B-3) and Namaka Lake (B-4).

Gas, food and washrooms can be found in Strathmore, 10 km further
east from Sadler's Slough along the Trans-Canada Highway.

ANDREW SLATER

B-3 Eagle Lake

Eagle Lake is situated about 40 km east of Calgary and a few kilometres southeast of the town of Strathmore. It is a large body of water,
measuring about 4.5 km in each direction, surrounded by agricultural
land. Impressive numbers of waterbirds and respectable numbers of
shorebirds are attracted to the lake during spring (early April to early
June) and fall (mid-July to early November) migration. There are also
large breeding populations of several species. It is used to some extent
by recreational boaters but many sections are shallow and weedy and
are left to the birds. Eagle Lake makes a good half-day trip from
Calgary, requiring from four to six hours return.

There are two main public access points: along an abandoned railway
embankment at the southwest corner and at Eagle Lake Park on the
eastern side. The southwestern access is the most recommended
because a larger area of the lake and shoreline is accessible, a good distance can be walked, there is less human disturbance and the sun is
behind you for most of the day.

Directions are given from the intersection of the Trans-Canada Highway and S.R. 817 in Strathmore (**km 0.0**). Head south on S.R. 817.
At 6.4 km, S.R. 560 (Glenmore Trail) enters from the west. (Those liv-
ing in southern Calgary may find S.R. 560 east a more direct route.)

9.6 km south of the Trans-Canada Highway turn left onto an east-west gravel road; this intersection is marked by a farm with a prominent machinery building. This road goes through an irrigated agricultural area, with several small sloughs which may contain good numbers of shorebirds and surface-feeding ducks during spring and fall migration. Small flocks of Sandhill Cranes and Greater White-fronted Geese are occasionally seen during September, either feeding in the stubble or passing overhead. Bald Eagles are sometimes seen in winter (November to March) perched in the tall poplars along irrigation canals, while a few Snowy Owls may be observed in the fields during the same period. The owls may be perched on the ground, on haybales, fenceposts or utility poles.

Turn left onto a gravel road marked with a yellow "No Exit" sign (14.4 km). Follow this north, observing the fields on either side carefully for geese, raptors or other birds in the stubble. Slow down as you approach the house just north of the Eagle Lake Ranching Company feedlot. If the hill looks muddy, it may be wise to park at the top. If road conditions are good, continue down the hill and park in the open area at the bottom. An abandoned railway embankment runs across the northern end of the parking area giving access to the west, past mudflats and reedbeds, to the southwest corner of the lake. From spring break-up to fall freeze-up this walk is almost always productive. Allow from one to two hours for the 3 km round trip. It is possible to drive your vehicle along the embankment as far as the middle of the lake. However, the road is wide enough for only one vehicle and as there is no turning space you either have to reverse or attempt a tedious and nerve-wracking turn on the embankment. Most birders will find the walk more enjoyable!

There is usually a large breeding colony of Eared Grebes to the south of the embankment and Forster's and Common Terns are often seen. Forster's Terns are most easily identified in August and September, when they assume the distinctive fall head-pattern. Soras are occasionally seen feeding in the open along the edges of the reedbeds on the south side. Oldsquaw sometimes occur in early November, just before freeze-up. Rarities recorded from the embankment include: Red-throated Loon, Black Scoter, Buff-breasted Sandpiper, Parasitic Jaeger and Sabine's Gull. In late September 1985, Alberta's first Little Gulls, an immature and an adult, first found at nearby Namaka Lake, were later observed here.

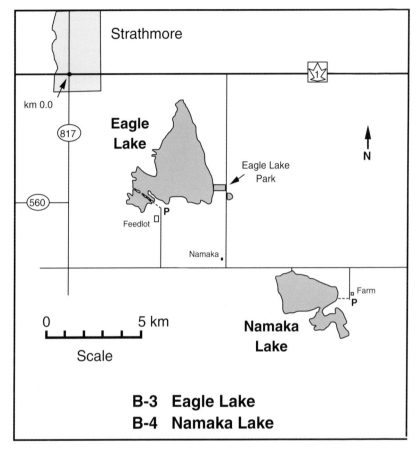

Strathmore

km 0.0

817

Eagle
Lake

560

Eagle Lake
Park

N

Feedlot

P

Namaka

Farm
P

0   5 km

Scale

Namaka
Lake

B-3   Eagle Lake
B-4   Namaka Lake

To continue to **Eagle Lake Park** on the east side of the lake, return to
the east-west gravel road and turn left. After going east for 3.2 km
turn left again; you are now heading north. (If you continue east you
will come to Namaka Lake, see site B-4.) Just before reaching the park
entrance on the left (approximately 3.5 km from the last turn), there is
a marshy slough on the right. This can be good for waterfowl and
shorebirds during migration; in summer, listen for Sora, Common
Snipe and Marsh Wren. (Note: Birders should stay on the road here as
the landowner does not allow access.) Upland Sandpiper has been
seen occasionally in the grassland west of the road. In summer, an
entrance fee is charged to take a vehicle into Eagle Lake Park, and the
gate is sometimes closed during the morning when the light is best for
viewing the lake. However, you can always park outside and walk in

to the shore. Many species of waterbirds and some shorebirds can be observed from here. Continue north for 6 km to the Trans-Canada Highway for the return to Calgary.

Gas, food and washrooms are available in Strathmore.

ANDREW SLATER

B-4 Namaka Lake

Namaka Lake is located approximately 50 km east of Calgary. It is one of the best locations for both waterfowl and shorebirds in the Region. In both spring and fall migration periods, the numbers and variety of waterbirds can be truly spectacular. It is a large, shallow, open body of water with the general overall appearance of two lakes connected by a narrow channel. The main patches of emergent vegetation are concentrated along the northwest shore and the borders of the lake south of the narrow channel. The land surrounding the lake is a mix of cultivated fields, fallow fields and pasture. A few scattered willows and poplars along the roads, and shelterbelts around nearby farmsteads are the only wooded habitats in the area. To date, 175 species of birds have been observed at Namaka Lake and in the surrounding fields.

Namaka Lake is a good half-day trip from Calgary, requiring from four to six hours for a return trip. If an all-day outing is planned, a visit to Namaka Lake could be combined with any one or more birding locations in the area such as McElroy Slough (B-5), Sadler's Slough (B-2), Bruce Lake (B-6), Eagle Lake (B-3), Dalemead Reservoir (B-1), or Wyndham-Carseland Provincial Park (B-1).

The starting point for directions to Namaka Lake is the junction of the Trans-Canada Highway and S.R. 817 in the town of Strathmore. Drive east on the Trans-Canada Highway for 8.2 km and watch for a large sign that says "EAGLE LAKE PARK". After you turn south, Eagle Lake is to your right. Drive south for about 10 km to a T-junction. Turn left and proceed east for approximately 2 km, where you will see a small brick building to your right. A short stop here may reward you with some good views of waterfowl. As you continue east you will see Namaka Lake on your right. Approximately 1.5 km from the last stop there is a gateway to the lake on the south side of the road, just west of the cattail beds and a small bridge over a drainage channel. Note where this access point is in case you would like to stop here on the way back, but for now continue east another 3 km before turning south on a gravel road. This road goes through a farmyard but is for public use. South of the buildings the road is earth, not gravel, and can be extremely slippery after rain or in early spring. Continue to the end and park in the parking lot.

As you walk westwards along the trail to the lake you will cross disturbed land consisting of cultivated fields, fallow fields and some grassland. In the fields and on the fenceposts, birds that may be seen during the breeding season (April to August) include Gray Partridge, Eastern Kingbird, Horned Lark, Vesper Sparrow, Savannah Sparrow and Western Meadowlark. Northern Harrier and Swainson's Hawk can usually be seen soaring or flying over these fields.

On reaching the shore it is advisable to scope the lake—many species of waterfowl can be observed from here. Depending on where you see good numbers of birds, you can either walk north along the lakeshore or head south; generally, a walk to the south is more rewarding. It is advisable to stop every few hundred metres to scan the lake and its shoreline. Along the shore you may see Great Blue Heron, Killdeer, American Avocet, Willet and Marbled Godwit. You will notice that the lake narrows near its southeast end and opens into a bay that is lined with dense stands of rushes, bulrushes and cattails. This is a good vantage point for observing grebes; American White Pelican; waterfowl; Wilson's Phalarope; Franklin's, Ring-billed and California Gulls; Common, Forster's and Black Terns; and blackbirds. By quietly moving along the shore at the edge of the emergent vegetation, you may hear and/or see American Bittern, Black-crowned Night-Heron, Sora, Common Snipe, Marsh Wren and Common Yellowthroat. From this point, you may either return the same way or take a direct route back across the fields to your vehicle. If you cross the fields, stop and listen in the lower areas where the grasses are taller, for Baird's and Le Conte's Sparrows. If you return the way you came and have the time available, stop at intervals to scope the lake again; this persistence is especially recommended during the spring and fall migration periods.

During spring and fall migration, the lake and adjacent fields attract
Common Loon; Tundra Swan; Greater White-fronted and Snow
Geese; Rough-legged Hawk; Sandhill Crane; a variety of shorebirds
including: Black-bellied and Semipalmated Plovers, Greater and Less-
er Yellowlegs, Hudsonian Godwit, Semipalmated, Least, Baird's,
Pectoral, and Stilt Sandpipers, Long-billed Dowitcher and Red-necked
Phalarope; Bonaparte's and Herring Gulls; swallows; American Pipit;
and Lapland Longspur. In November as freeze-up approaches, Bald
Eagles may be seen in the area.

Rarities that have been observed during fall migration at Namaka
Lake include: Greater Scaup; Oldsquaw; Lesser Golden-Plover; Ruddy
Turnstone; Dunlin; Buff-breasted Sandpiper; Red Phalarope; Parasitic
Jaeger; Little, Glaucous-winged, Glaucous and Sabine's Gulls; and
Caspian and Arctic Terns.

Gas, food and washrooms are available in Strathmore.

HAROLD W. PINEL

B-5 McElroy Slough Driving Route

This short route is suitable for those birders who have only a few
hours to spare and would like to see some waterfowl or shorebirds.
The best birding months are mid-April to June in the spring and
August to November in the fall.

The route begins at the intersection of 17 Ave SE (Hwy 1A) and
68 St SE in Calgary (**km 0.0**). On the southwest corner of this intersection is the **Forest Lawn stormwater retention pond**. In recent years,
the large numbers of over-wintering Mallards have attracted Gyrfalcon and other raptors, especially in November and December.

As you drive east along Hwy 1A, watch for Swainson's and Red-tailed
Hawks on fenceposts and Great Horned Owl along the hedgerows. In
winter, Snowy Owl is occasionally reported from here. If moisture
conditions are right, there will be a series of small sloughs along the

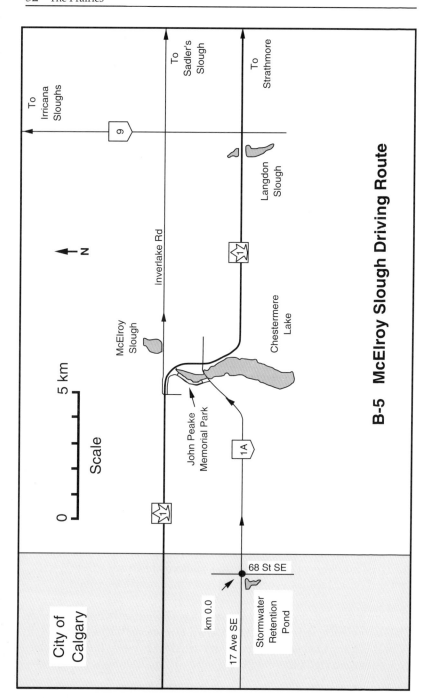

B-5 McElroy Slough Driving Route

road. In spring, watch for American Avocet but stopping here can be difficult due to the steady traffic. After driving for 8.5 km turn left onto West Park Drive (gravel-surfaced), just before the Chestermere Lake Bridge. One kilometre after the turn, the entrance to John Peake Memorial Park is reached on your right. An entry fee is charged in summer; at other times there may be a barrier to prevent vehicular access. Either drive slowly along the road, or park and walk the trail. The lake is often good in early spring for waterfowl; Common Loon and most species of grebes are easily seen here. In May, watch for American Avocet; Marbled Godwit; Sanderling; Semipalmated, Least, Baird's and Pectoral Sandpipers; and Long-billed Dowitcher. Hudson-ian Godwit is regularly observed but you need to be lucky. Clay-colored, Vesper and Savannah Sparrows should be seen along the fence on the other side of the road.

Continue driving until the Trans-Canada Highway is reached (11 km). Carefully cross this busy divided highway and follow Inverlake Road (gravel-surfaced) east for 2 km to **McElroy Slough,** a small irrigation reservoir, on the north side of the road. It can be excellent for most species of waterfowl. Early migrations of Tundra Swans stopover here, along with hundreds of Canada Geese and the occasional Greater White-fronted Goose. It is good for diving ducks—great rafts are seen regularly. Watch for White-winged Scoter and other difficult to see waterfowl around Calgary; Eurasian Wigeon has occurred on several occasions. On May 3, 1992 a male Tufted Duck (the first for the province) and a Caspian Tern were observed here.

Continuing on, a small slough is reached on the left at 16.7 km. This begins as a narrow channel paralleling the road and then opens up into a shallow marsh. Wilson's Phalarope is often found in the deep-er channel, with other types of shorebirds enjoying the shallow slough behind. This area can be excellent for Black-bellied Plover, Long-billed Curlew and, depending on water depth, most of the peeps.

At 20.5 km another intermittent slough is reached which can also be good for waterfowl and shorebirds. At 21.9 km the road intersects Hwy 9. At this point you can either turn right and drive a further 3.3 km to the Trans-Canada Highway for the journey back to Calgary, or continue on to other locations. A left turn will take you north towards Irricana (B-6); continuing east on the gravel road for 9.8 km will bring you to the Sadler's Slough road (B-2); or turn left at the Trans-Canada Highway for Eagle Lake (B-3) and Namaka Lake (B-4).

DAVE ELPHINSTONE

B-6 The Irricana Area and Bruce Lake Driving Route

The "Irricana circuit" is a driving loop through good waterfowl and shorebird habitat on the prairies northeast of Calgary. It includes two large sloughs, numerous smaller ones and the northern end of Bruce Lake. The larger bodies of water are deep enough to be good for birds even in very dry years. The best time is from late April to the end of May but most species occur in good numbers throughout the summer, and interesting birds can usually be found anytime from spring thaw (early April) to freeze-up (end of October). The loop begins 40 km from Calgary at Keoma and is 70 km long, for a total distance of 150 km round trip from the city limits. 40 km are on good gravel roads (dusty in dry weather); the other roads are hard-surfaced. Allow 4 to 5 hours for the loop, plus an hour round trip from Calgary, to give lots of time for stops.

There are many birds that can be seen on the Irricana circuit which are not specifically associated with water, and stopping to look and listen at regular intervals along the fields away from the sloughs can often turn up interesting species. In April, May, September and October (see the Abundance Chart for the best times), look for migrating Rough-legged Hawks, Townsend's Solitaires (uncommon) and flocks of American Pipits, Lapland Longspurs and Snow Buntings (these flocks often alight in stubble fields). Sandhill Cranes can occasionally be seen in August and September. Check hawk nests in April and May to see if Great Horned Owls are using them. Watch the roadside for Gray Partridge (all months) and the occasional Ring-necked Pheasant. Swainson's Hawk is the most common raptor in summer, but Northern Harrier and Red-tailed Hawk are usually seen as well. During the breeding season (May-July), listen for Horned Lark, Savannah

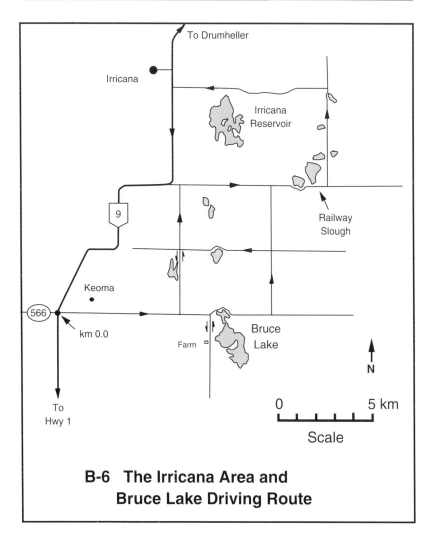

To Drumheller

Irricana

Irricana
Reservoir

9

Railway
Slough

Keoma

566

km 0.0

Farm

Bruce
Lake

N

To
Hwy 1

0   5 km

Scale

**B-6   The Irricana Area and
Bruce Lake Driving Route**

Sparrow (the most common sparrow in this area), Vesper Sparrow, Western Meadowlark, and perhaps a Sprague's Pipit overhead. Clay-colored Sparrow can often be found where there are bushes or trees. Long-billed Curlew may be seen in several places. Shrikes (Logger-head in summer and Northern in Winter) are uncommon, but are sometimes seen; check the fence lines, and any other prominent spots which a shrike might use for a lookout. During April and perhaps September, the two species may overlap and any shrike seen in those months should be scrutinized carefully. Almost every wet area has Red-winged and Yellow-headed Blackbirds, and many of them have Common Snipe winnowing overhead.

Directions to the start of the driving loop are given from the traffic light at 16 Ave (Hwy 1) and 68 St NE in Calgary. From here, drive 20.2 km east on Hwy 1 to the junction with Hwy 9. The junction is marked by signs for Drumheller and the Royal Tyrrell Museum of Palaeontology. Turn left onto Hwy 9 and go north to the intersection at the first bend, 19.5 km from Hwy 1. Turn right, towards Keoma (this point will be called "the Keoma turnoff" for the rest of this description). There is a directional sign on Hwy 9 for Keoma. The driving loop begins at the Keoma turnoff, so take an odometer reading or reset your tripmeter here.

If you have time while driving to the start of the loop, there is a stop along Hwy 1 which is usually worthwhile. This is **Langdon Slough,** located on the right (south) side of the highway, one kilometre before (west of) the junction with Hwy 9 (see Map B-5). It is easily viewed from the car and usually has numerous ducks. It can also be very good for migrating shorebirds if the water level is right. Birding here is usually best in spring but in the late summer of 1989 White-rumped Sandpiper and Black-necked Stilt were observed. In very dry years, however, it can almost disappear.

Starting from the **Keoma turnoff** at Hwy 9 (**km 0.0**), drive east towards Bruce Lake. Short-eared Owls are occasionally seen along this stretch. (Keoma Slough is 2.4 km from the Keoma turnoff, but it is difficult to stop safely. All species there are likely to be seen again later in the loop). When **Bruce Lake** can be seen ahead on the right (8.1 km from the Keoma turnoff), turn right on the small gravel road and drive south for one kilometre. Stop, listen and watch for Baird's and Grasshopper Spar-rows in this area. Check the lake on the left side. A Snowy Egret was seen on this part of the lakeshore on the 10 and 11 May, 1983. Turn at the first farmhouse, return to the road junction (now 11 km from the Keoma turnoff), and turn right. Bruce Lake comes close to the road in two bays which are separated from each other along the road by a short bit of land. Birds seen here include Common Loon; all five local grebes; American White Pelican (irregular summer visitors to the west bay); Double-crested Cormorant; Great Blue Heron; Black-crowned Night-Heron (these are usually seen either in a marshy area on either side of the road as you approach the second (eastern) bay, or else along the far or far left shore of the second bay; check the lowest branches of the bushes that overhang the water); and Tundra Swan in migration. Ducks include all the local surface-feeding species plus Common Goldeneye, Bufflehead, and Hooded, Common, and Red-breasted (April-May) Mergansers. Sora occur in the reeds along the first (western) bay, and several species of shorebirds may be seen, although the shoreline along the road is not well-suited for them. Bonaparte's, Ring-billed, California and Herring Gulls, and Common, Forster's (occasionally) and Black Terns can all occur. A Black-legged Kittiwake was photographed here on June 6, 1982. Around the lake watch for Ring-necked Pheasant; Eastern Kingbird; swallows; Marsh Wren in the reeds along the western bay; Yellow Warbler; Common Yellowthroat at the western bay; Yellow-rumped and possibly other warblers on migration.

Follow the road along the north shore of Bruce Lake to the point where the road leaves the lake (12 km from the Keoma turnoff). The route from this point is on good gravel roads. Stay on this road a further 2.4 km straight east, then turn left (north) and drive 3.2 km to a stop sign. A Sage Thrasher was seen near the white farmhouse along this stretch on May 19, 1986.

Turn left at the crossroads and drive west for 2.8 km to a large pond on the left side of the road. This is good for grebes and ducks, being a particularly likely place for Ring-necked Duck in early summer. On the right side is a cattail marsh which is alive with blackbirds. This is one of the few places in the Region where Common Grackle is frequently seen. Beyond the pond and marsh is a wooded area which is on private land, but birding from the road may turn up migrating warblers, Great Horned Owl and other woodland species. Cooper's Hawk has nested here.

5 km from the last junction (22.6 km), turn left and drive south for about one kilometre to a large slough on the west side of the road. One of the most unlikely coincidences of local birding took place here. Spoonbill Sandpiper was reported and well-described at this location on two occasions: two birds on May 19, 1984 and one on May 9, 1992. The field between the slough and the road may contain Baird's Sparrow in summer and the marshy area past the southern tip of the slough (1.9 km south of the last junction) has had Le Conte's Sparrow nesting. Both species sing from small bushes and tall grass stems.

Turn around and drive 1.9 km north, cross the east-west road you were on previously and continue 2.3 km further north. Stop here and listen for Sprague's Pipit and Baird's Sparrow. The pipit's flight song can often be heard from early May to late July and careful watching may find the bird high up, a speck against the sky.

0.9 km further north (3.2 km from the last crossroads and 29.6 km from the Keoma turnoff) you come to a T-junction, where you should turn right (Hwy 9 is to the left). Continue east for 4 km and watch for Bobolink (rare in the Region).

5.2 km from the last turn is the first of several sloughs. It is close to the road and easily viewed from the car. Also check the small sloughs on the south side of the road along this stretch. Birds seen on the large slough include Tundra Swan on migration in April, Greater Scaup (occasionally), Surf Scoter (rarely), White-winged Scoter, Barrow's Goldeneye (April), Long-billed Dowitcher, and Wilson's Phalarope. Eurasian Wigeon has been recorded here. As the road rounds the edge of this slough, watch for a small shallow slough on the right (south side), close to the road. This can be good for migrating shorebirds; Dunlin has been seen here.

Another large slough (often called **Railway Slough**) comes into view suddenly, on the left as you top the crest of a small rise (36.7 km). This is the old railway right-of–way, but the tracks are long since gone. Probably the best view is obtained from here, but be careful to park safely to avoid danger from cars coming up the rise from either side. The main part of Railway Slough is not so easily viewed as the previous slough, but can still be scoped. A shallow extension does come close to the road however; this can be good for wading birds. Many species can be expected at the appropriate season, including (rarely) Upland Sandpiper. American Bittern has been seen here.

From the crest of the rise at Railway Slough, continue one kilometre east to a road junction. At the time of writing there is a sign nailed to a fencepost on the far left corner of the junction saying "Bull Test Station". Turn left (north) here. There are two or three small sloughs on the left shortly after the junction (before the farmhouse), and the larger of these may add birds missed on the previous sloughs. The last section of this road (after the farmhouse) is the best section of the route for Upland Sandpiper. Also, watch and listen for Swainson's,

Red-tailed and Ferruginous Hawks; Mourning Dove; Sprague's Pipit; and McCown's and Chestnut-collared Longspurs. 4.1 km north of the "Bull Test" junction, the road passes an alkaline slough. This is good for ducks and shorebirds; Eurasian Wigeon has been seen here.

This is the last slough of the loop. Continue north to a red natural gas pipeline valve on your right (42.6 km). Turn left (west) and drive 7.3 km back to Hwy 9. Turn left (south); 16 km takes you back to the Keoma junction, and a further 19.5 km back to Hwy 1. Turn right on Hwy 1 for Calgary. One kilometre after turning onto Hwy 1 there is a northern extension of Langdon Slough on your right. This can be good for shorebirds, but traffic on the highway can be bothersome. Alternatively, you may prefer to turn right from Hwy 9 onto Inverlake Road 16.4 km south of the Keoma turnoff (see B-5, the McElroy Slough Driving Route).

Gas, food and washrooms are available in the town of Irricana.

WILLIAM J.F. WILSON

B-7 The Drumheller Area

The badlands topography of the Red Deer Valley forms a dramatic contrast to the gently rolling grain fields to the south and west of Drumheller. Vigorous erosion has created a series of deeply incised, winding gullies (locally known as coulees) leading from the deep clay sediments of the surrounding area into the main river valley. Barren slopes and hot dry summers would at first glance seem to preclude productive birding but where canyon or coulee walls give protection from the sun and the drying effects of winter Chinook winds, thicker vegetation does grow, providing cover for birds and nesting sites. A variety of dry land species can be found here, with few nesting away from the river valleys and coulees. Birding is most rewarding during June and early July, in the morning before the daily heat build-up. A full day will be required.

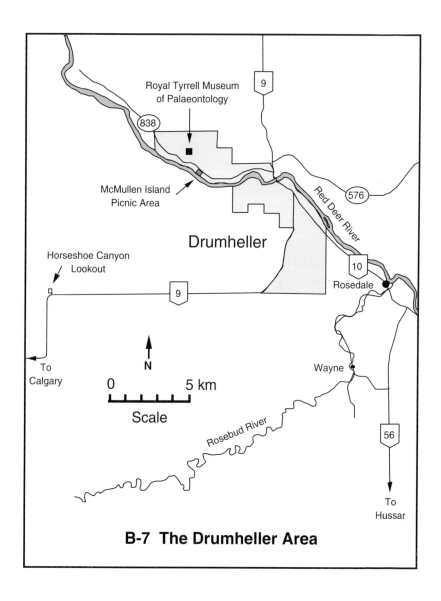

B-7 The Drumheller Area

The quickest route to Drumheller from Calgary takes about 90 minutes
(130 km). Head north on Deerfoot Trail (Hwy 2) from the 64 Ave NE
interchange (**km 0.0**) in NE Calgary, and take the Hwy 72 exit
(31.3 km). This exit is easy to miss—watch for large Tyrrell Museum
road signs of white letters on a brown background. Follow Hwy 72
east through Beiseker to the junction with Hwy 9 (65.5 km). Continue
east through this junction. This puts you on Hwy 9, which you should
continue to follow east towards Drumheller. Carefully examine each
flying raptor since there is the possibility of seeing Turkey Vulture;
Ferruginous Hawks may also stray into the area from the Hanna
region to the east. Gray Partridge, Ring-necked Pheasant and Sharp-
tailed Grouse (occasionally) may be seen along the roadsides.

Your first opportunity to view the spectacular badlands scenery is at
the Horseshoe Canyon lookout (113.2 km and immediately east of a
curve in the road). Extreme erosion of the soft clay valley walls by the
occasional heavy shower has carved rounded mounds of layered sediments. Few birds are evident along the edge of the canyon in summer,
except for Black-capped Chickadee. From the parking lot many "unofficial" trails lead down to the canyon bottom. These trails should not
be used, however, as the soft sediment is too easily eroded—there are
other places where hiking is less damaging to the scenery.

In deep coulees where there are stands of spruce, birding is often more
productive in winter. The local Christmas Bird Count, centred on
Horseshoe Canyon, regularly lists Downy Woodpecker, Pileated Woodpecker, Pine Grosbeak, Bohemian Waxwing and Great Horned Owl.

Continuing on Hwy 9, at the south end of Drumheller (129 km) is a
Tourist Information booth, open daily during summer from 9:00 a.m.
to 9:00 p.m. It can provide an excellent brochure on the attractions of
the Drumheller Valley, including the 48 km Dinosaur Trail driving
loop, which passes several areas of badlands and riparian woodland
of interest to birders. Visitors to the Calgary area are encouraged to
plan an outing to the **Royal Tyrrell Museum of Palaeontology**
(entrance fee). Opened in 1985, this facility is designed not only to
showcase the abundant Cretaceous fossils recovered from southern
Alberta but also to give an understanding of the broad sweep of evo-
lution. There is much to interest a birder; incurable listers will enjoy
the cast of *Archaeopteryx*. The museum is situated on the Dinosaur
Trail driving loop leading west from Drumheller, on the north side of

the Red Deer River. Visits to this facility should be planned for the afternoon birding doldrum period when air-conditioning will be most appreciated. Expect to spend a minimum of 2 hours at the museum if you are interested in this subject. To reach the museum turn north-west at the intersection of Highways 9, 10 and 56 (129.9 km), then turn north at the traffic light on 2 St W, cross the river, then turn west at North Dinosaur Trail (S.R. 838). Make note of the McMullen Island Picnic Area (136 km) and continue to the museum entrance (137.2 km).

There is spectacular badland terrain immediately outside the museum, where short hiking trails allow the visitor to explore the habitat. Say's Phoebe and Brewer's Blackbird nest here while American Kestrels often roost on the mounds. The best morning birding in the area how-ever, is at the **McMullen Island Picnic Area** in Midland Provincial Park. Massive cottonwood trees dominate the site with an extensive thick Red-osier Dogwood shrub undergrowth providing ideal habitat for White-tailed Deer, birds and mosquitoes. A network of short winding trails provides opportunities to closely approach park birds. Nesting species include American Kestrel, Western Kingbird, Swain-son's Thrush, Brown Thrasher and Yellow-breasted Chat (rare). A pair of Pileated Woodpeckers used a utility pole in which to raise a brood in 1989. This location is also good during migration periods. A Fork-tailed Flycatcher was observed here on June 1, 1988.

Deep ravines or coulees which join the main valley are the other reli-able source of bird sightings. Due to heat and rapid evaporation, shrubbery such as willows and poplar trees are often present only on north-facing slopes. The dense understory is invariably a combination of Buckbrush and wild rose. These small groves attract nesting Swain-son's Hawks, House Wrens, Yellow Warblers and Rufous-sided Towhees. Prickly pear cactus grows on the generally barren south-facing slopes; it flowers at the end of June. If there are sandstone ledges one may see Prairie Falcon, Say's Phoebe, Cliff Swallow, Rock Wren and Mountain Bluebird. Gravel pits cut into these slopes are prime locations for Bank Swallows. Elevation change is rapid but hik-ers are usually able to follow well-worn paths created by Mule Deer. Most of the coulees are on private land, so permission to enter should be obtained from the landowner.

A nearby birding location offering close proximity to steep coulee banks which can be birded from the roadside, is the **Rosebud River**

valley. During the breeding season Spotted Sandpiper, Mourning Dove, Least Flycatcher, Cliff Swallow, Mountain Bluebird, Gray Catbird, Cedar Waxwing and Yellow Warbler can be found here. Bullock's Oriole, the rare subspecies for southern Alberta, has been seen here. Starting in Drumheller at the intersection of Highways 9, 10 & 56 **(km 0.0),** head southeast on Hwy 10/56 to the community of Rosedale. Turn right (south) at the outdoor skating rink (6.7 km) and head for Wayne. Follow the meandering road, crossing over nine bridges. At the tenth bridge (12.9 km), and just after the "Last Chance Saloon" in Wayne, a deep coulee intersects the valley from the east. Turn east on the gravel road and begin a fairly steep climb out of the main valley. The sparse shrubbery and sage along the steep slopes may produce Lark Sparrow. At Hwy 56 (paved, 15.4 km) turn right (south) and continue to the intersection with S.R. 561 (53.4 km), near Hussar. (Caution: THE GRAVEL ROAD UP FROM WAYNE IS HAZ-ARDOUS WHEN WET; it would be better in this case to turn around at Wayne, drive back to Rosedale, turn right (southeast) on Hwy 10/56 to Cambria, and then right again on Hwy 56, rejoining the route out of Wayne after a few kilometres.)   Follow S.R. 561 (paved) west until it connects with the Trans-Canada Highway (83.9 km), 20 km east of Strathmore.

Watch fenceposts in the Hussar area for Short-eared Owl. Roadmaps show a large waterbody at the intersection of Hwys 56 and 561, known as Deadhorse Lake. It was an important migration stopover for shorebirds a decade ago, but several years of low rainfall have caused it to dry up completely. Hwy 56 itself offers few birding opportunities, except in April, when seasonal sloughs formed by spring runoff attract migrating Tundra Swans and other waterfowl.

There are some precautions which visitors to the Drumheller area should consider. The soft clay in the Red Deer River valley and its tributaries is pleasant to walk on when dry, but is both slippery and sticky when wet. All gravel or dirt roads with steep gradients should be avoided during and after a rain. Hiking is hazardous when slopes are wet—remember the cacti! Ticks are possible in May and June; rattlesnakes are extremely unlikely.

Full tourist facilities are available in Drumheller. It is best to pack a lunch, however, and enjoy a picnic at McMullen Island or along the Dinosaur Trail.

For those approaching the Drumheller area from the east, an alternative route from the Trans-Canada Highway will save some time. About 19 km west of Bassano, turn right onto Hwy 56 and drive 37 km north to the Wayne turnoff (marked by a green and white sign), passing the junction with S.R. 561 on the way. If the weather is poor (i.e. raining or it has rained recently) it is recommended you continue north on Hwy 56 to Cambria, rather than attempting the steep access road down to Wayne.

ROSS DICKSON

B-8 Frank Lake

Frank Lake, situated about 50 km southeast of Calgary, is a shallow slough typical of the grasslands of southern Alberta. Species to be expected are ducks, prairie marsh birds and shorebirds. It has varied from a large lake with nesting American White Pelicans (in the 1950s) to a dry lake bed (in the 1980s). Currently, it is being fed water via an industrial pipeline from High River. Depending upon future circumstances, Frank Lake may again become a large water body. Unfortunately, many grassland species no longer occur in the area due to its increasingly intensive cultivation.

Directions are given from the southern edge of Calgary where Hwy 2 intersects with Hwy 22X (the Marquis of Lorne Trail). At this intersection (**km 0.0**) proceed south on Hwy 2. The highway passes through a varied area of native grassland, aspen clumps and croplands. The bird life is not very rich but is typical of this part of Alberta. At the junction with Hwy 23 (41.3 km), take the exit east towards Vulcan. For the next 6 km the highway goes primarily through croplands. At several points Baird's Sparrow can be found in small patches of low lying native vegetation.

At 47.3 km the highway makes a 90° turn to the north. As you approach this corner SLOW DOWN and watch for a dirt track that continues to the east. This wide track is rutted and quite slick when wet. Almost as soon as you leave the paved highway there is a gate in

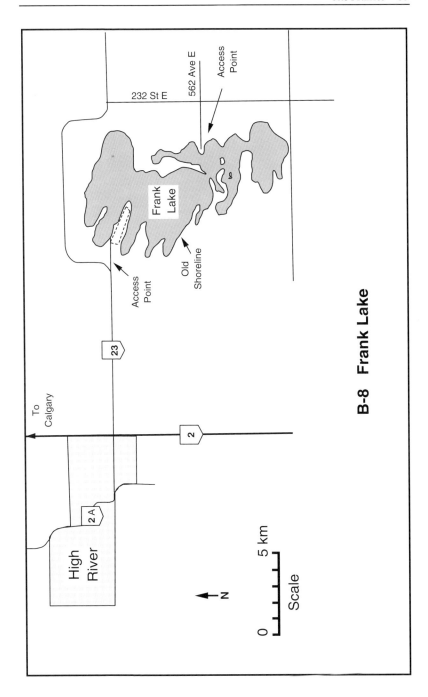

B-8 Frank Lake

a barbed wire fence (Gate #1). After a short distance there is a second fencewire gate (Gate #2). It is best to park here and continue on foot. The trail now divides with one part heading east and the other south along the east side of the fence line. Take the trail heading east. To the south is a grainfield, to the north part of the old lake bottom. During the nesting season Upland Sandpiper, Sprague's Pipit, Savannah Sparrow, Baird's Sparrow and Western Meadowlark can be found here.

The water and marsh begin at the power line. The trail then follows the old shoreline for about 2 km before eventually curving west. Most of the birds characteristic of this area may be found in this section. During the nesting season watch for Pied-billed, Horned, and Eared Grebes; American Bittern; Black-crowned Night-Heron; Canada Goose; Green-winged Teal; Northern Pintail; Blue-winged Teal; Cinnamon Teal; Northern Shoveler; Gadwall; American Wigeon; Canvasback; Redhead; Lesser Scaup; Ruddy Duck; Northern Harrier; Swainson's Hawk; Sora; American Coot; Killdeer; American Avocet; Willet; Marbled Godwit; Common Snipe; Wilson's Phalarope; Franklin's Gull; Forster's and Black Terns; Marsh Wren; and Red-winged and Yellow-headed Blackbirds. Black-necked Stilt nested here in 1991. During migration, especially fall (August and September), one can expect many other species. In the past more than twenty shorebird species have been recorded.

When the trail begins to head west and again passes under the power line, you have the choice of either going back along the lake shore or taking the trail heading north along the fence line to Gate #2. However, as this shortcut is usually devoid of bird life, it is definitely more interesting to retrace your route.

The southeastern shore of Frank Lake can be accessed by turning right from the dirt track and continuing on Hwy 23. The highway abruptly changes direction several times, skirting around the old shoreline. After 8.3 km turn right (south) onto 232 St E (gravel-surfaced and marked by a small white sign for High River Colony). Continue for a further 3.3 km, then turn right again onto 562 Ave E, marked by a yellow "No Exit" sign. This small road becomes a single lane dirt track. In dry driving conditions it can be followed for 2.3 km to the edge of the old shoreline. Here, an earthen causeway provides a good vantage point for scoping the lake.

Gas, food and washrooms are available in the town of High River, on Hwy 23 to the west of Hwy 2.

WAYNE W. SMITH

B-9 McGregor Lake

Surrounded by intensively cultivated grainfields, this 32 km-long reservoir is the largest permanent waterbody between Calgary and the U.S. border. It is an important staging area for waterfowl, the spring and fall migration periods being the best times for birding. By road, McGregor Lake is about 120 km southeast of Calgary. Directions are given from the entrance to Wyndham-Carseland Provincial Park (see route B-1).

From the park gate, drive south on Hwy 24 for 39 km to the intersection with S.R. 542. This is preceded by a large sign pointing to the Lake McGregor Recreation Area. (Note: you must turn east onto S.R. 542 about 50 m BEFORE the stop sign, which is actually at the junction with Hwy 23.)   After driving another 24.1 km, and just after the intersection with S.R. 842, watch for a stone cairn on the right-hand side of the road. This marks the entrance to the recreation area and access to the reservoir. Along the route Swainson's Hawk and Horned Lark are the common species, but watch also for the occasional Golden Eagle, Long-billed Curlew or Short-eared Owl. An American Badger may scurry across the road.

At McGregor Lake species of note to watch for include Tundra Swan; Greater White-fronted, Snow, and Ross' Geese; and Sandhill Crane (spring). Large flocks of Western Grebes can also occur. When looking for geese in spring, check both the fields and shoreline at the northern end of the lake. Bald Eagles occur in both spring and fall, attracted by the abundant ground squirrels and waterfowl. Small numbers of such local rarities as Ruddy Turnstone and Red Knot have been recorded at the northern end of the lake in the second half of May. In spring and summer Sprague's Pipit can be heard singing in the northwest corner. In summer, both McCown's and Chestnut-

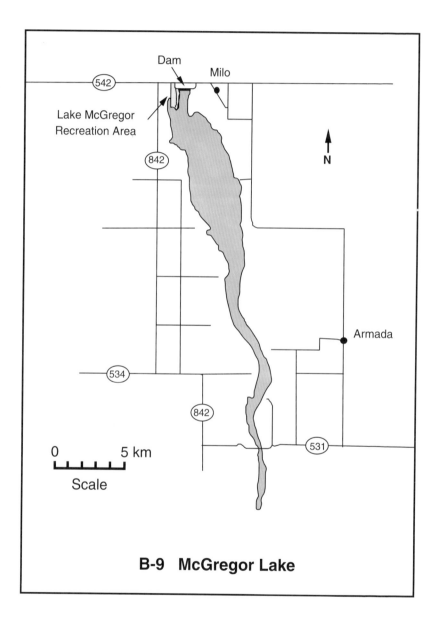

B-9   McGregor Lake

collared Longspurs can be found in the rolling native grassland on the east side of the lake. These patches of grassland are also excellent in winter for Golden Eagle, Prairie Falcon and Snowy Owl.

Shoreline birding is easiest at the recreation area. Here, a well-maintained service road on top of the dam, one kilometre in length, allows an elevated view of the marsh to the north and the reservoir to the south. During the breeding season the marsh features Black-crowned Night-Heron, a dozen species of ducks, American Avocet, Willet, both Common and Black Terns, and Yellow-headed Blackbird. Eurasian Wigeon has been observed here in early spring. The short driving loop around the marsh is recommended rather than attempting a turnaround on the dam. Even though the lake is a centre for recreation, dozens of American White Pelicans may be seen in summer, either loafing on the small island or fishing near the boat launch ramp. The unpaved road down to the boat ramp can be very muddy after rain.

More of the water may be viewed by driving the system of gravelled roads surrounding the lake. These can be dusty when dry, slippery when wet. Lighting conditions are best if this is done in a clockwise direction. From the park cairn continue east on S.R. 542, through Milo, and then take the first road south (3.6 km). It can be worthwhile trying each intersecting road for views of the lake. If you are unsure of access, ask at the nearest farm. The dirt road to the lake at the "bend", where the gravel road heads east, gives access to a section of shoreline near which Greater White-fronted and Ross' Geese have been reported in fall. From the bend, continue on the gravel road to the almost derelict hamlet of Armada. The shore can be accessed from here. Head west for about 5 km, past a "No Exit" sign, to an ungated pasture inhabited by pump jacks. If the dirt road in the field is dry, follow it until you can get better looks at the lake, then walk over to the shore. Flocks of Snow Geese can usually be seen from here during the second half of October.

After returning to the "No Exit" sign, turn south at the nearby intersection; S.R. 531 (paved) is reached after 6.4 km. Turn right (west) here. Watch for a small parking area located on the south side of the highway and the eastern shore of the reservoir. This is a good vantage point. In fall, the water immediately south of the causeway is the last to freeze; some late migrants may linger here. Continue west along the highway, then turn north onto S.R. 842 which is also marked by a sign for Milo.

For the return journey to Calgary from the McGregor Lake cairn, an alternative route is to head back along S.R. 542 to the main intersection and to then continue west on Hwy 23 for 43 km to Hwy 2. From the High River interchange it is 35 km to Hwy 22X in south Calgary. Although you are unlikely to see birds other than Gray Partridge or Red-tailed and Swainson's Hawks, the mountain scenery along the western horizon is spectacular at any season. A northward jog in Hwy 23 indicates the presence of Frank Lake (see site B-8).

Gas is available at the intersection of Hwy 23 and S.R. 542. Milo has a cafe (closed Mondays). There are pit toilets at the recreation area. In spring and summer take plenty of bug repellent. During the fall hunting season, only Sunday visits are recommended.

ROSS DICKSON

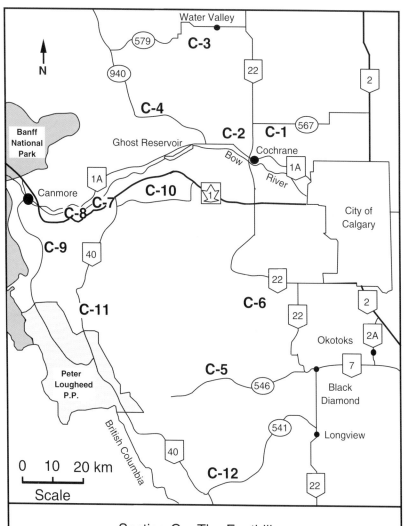

N

Water Valley

579

C-3

940

C-4

22

2

Banff National Park

Ghost Reservoir

C-2

C-1

567

Cochrane

Bow

River

1A

1A

Canmore

C-8

C-7

C-10

1

City of Calgary

C-9

40

C-11

22

22

C-6

2

Okotoks

2A

Peter Lougheed P.P.

C-5

546

Black Diamond

7

British Columbia

541

Longview

0 10 20 km

Scale

40

C-12

22

Section C: The Foothills

C-1 Big Hill Springs P. P.
C-2 Grand Valley Road
C-3 Water Valley Area
C-4 Forestry Trunk Road
C-5 Sheep River Valley
C-6 Brown-Lowery R. A.

C-7 Bow Valley P. P.
C-8 Lac Des Arcs
C-9 Smith-Dorrien/ Spray Trail
C-10 Sibbald Creek Trail
C-11 The Kananaskis Valley
C-12 The Highwood Valley

C-1 Big Hill Springs Provincial Park

Big Hill Springs Provincial Park is located at the lower end of Big Spring Coulee, approximately 25 km northwest of Calgary. The park is quite small, covering only 26 hectares, but the close proximity of an extensive marsh complex and a lake formed by the damming of Bighill Creek add to the birding possibilities. The most rewarding months for birding are May through August; the area can be covered in half a day or an evening.

From the intersection of Crowchild Trail (Hwy 1A) and Nosehill Drive in northwest Calgary head west on Hwy 1A for 10.5 km. Turn right on Lochend Road (S.R. 766) and drive north for 11 km to the junction with S.R. 567. Turn left (west) on S.R. 567 and continue for 3.3 km to the park access road. Turn left (south) on the access road and continue to the end, parking in the parking lot beyond the Texas gate.

An interpretive trail, 1.6 km in length, begins at the stone fire pit. Good use has been made of the varied terrain, the trail first paralleling the moist and shady streambed, then rising through grassland and sheltered mixed woodland on the coulee wall before dropping back down to the parking lot. A respectable spring migration can usually be observed here. Species seen in recent years have included Tennessee, Orange-crowned, Blackpoll and MacGillivray's Warblers, American Redstart, Northern Waterthrush and Western Tanager. Nesting species include Western Wood-Pewee, Least Flycatcher, Eastern Phoebe, Gray Catbird, Cedar Waxwing, Yellow Warbler, Clay-colored, Vesper and Song Sparrows, and Pine Siskin. A pair of Red-naped Sapsuckers has nested in a poplar beside the trail for several years. Listen in early spring for Northern Saw-whet Owl. Ruffed Grouse is more likely to be heard than seen. In August, check the flower-filled meadow just before the tufa deposit for Rufous Hummingbird. Prairie Falcon breeds in the area and is most likely to be seen from the access road. In late March and early April concentrations of Bald Eagles regularly occur near the park. In severe winters, check open areas of the spring (especially at the observation deck by the tufa deposit) for American Dipper. The soils are extremely thin in the park and are easily eroded—it is important that you stay on the established trail. The park is a popular family recreation area, it is best to bird here early in the morning.

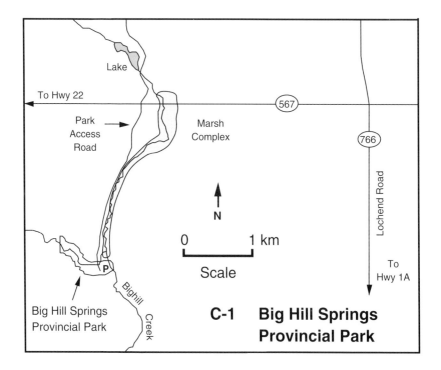

C-1   **Big Hill Springs Provincial Park**

The marsh complex, which has been formed by the action of beavers on Bighill Creek, parallels the access road from the highway to the Texas gate. In May, this is an excellent location for really close observation of most surface-feeding ducks, including Cinnamon Teal. Spotted Sandpiper, Common Snipe and, in some years Wilson's Phalarope, nest here. Solitary Sandpiper is regular during migration. Sora are abundant and in July, with a little patience and by using your vehicle as a blind, it is possible to watch the adults feeding their young, just metres away. This is a popular foraging area for Great Blue Heron, up to five have been seen on occasion. Belted Kingfisher is an uncommon visitor—check the powerline wire near the Texas gate. A major interest at the Big Hill Springs marsh complex is a small colony of Sharp-tailed Sparrows. They can be heard and seen from the park access road, but the most favourable viewing location is from S.R. 567. Go east from the intersection and watch for the culvert carrying Bighill Creek beneath the highway. To the east of the culvert is "the" best viewing area. The shoulder is almost non-existent but it is possible to pull far enough off the highway to use a small vehicle as a blind. If traffic is heavy, it would be safer to park on the access road and walk. The sparrows arrive at the end of May. Listen for a strange hissing sound reminiscent of hot metal being plunged into water. The sound doesn't carry very far—so if you can hear a Sharp-tailed Sparrow, you should also be able to see it. Check the middle strand of fencewire beside the shrub and the scattered low bushes in the wet meadow. After singing briefly, the Sharp-tailed Sparrow flits to another favoured perch nearby and repeats the performance. Le Conte's Sparrows (bzeeee-zip) can be found here too, but they prefer the moister area with taller grass, west of the culvert.

Yellow Rails were discovered here in 1990 and have returned in subsequent years. In order to safeguard this fragile habitat and such local rarities as Yellow Rail and Sharp-tailed Sparrow, it is vital that birders restrict their viewing to the highway and park access road. Entering a wetland during the nesting season for the purpose of flushing such species is totally unacceptable birding behaviour. Not only is it harrassment but it can also lead to nesting failure and abandonment of the site.

To reach the lake, take the gravel road heading north opposite the park access road. It can be worthwhile checking out the marsh on this side of the highway too. The gravel road first curves uphill and then skirts around the lake. Common Loon, Ring-necked Duck, Surf Scoter, White-winged Scoter, Barrow's Goldeneye and Hooded Merganser have been observed here in late April and May. A White-faced Ibis played hide and seek with birders here from May 12–14, 1990. Breeding species include Pied-billed, Horned and Red-necked Grebes, Canada Goose, most of the prairie ducks, Common Snipe, Black Tern and Yellow-headed Blackbird. In some years, post-breeding male Ring-necked Ducks summer here. A good location for scoping the lake is from half-way up the hill, where the gravel road widens sufficiently to park safely. This is also a good vantage point to watch for raptors. Sprague's Pipit can often be heard singing above the dry hillside. Upland Sandpiper regularly occurs in this and other fescue grasslands in the area; in wet years Baird's Sparrow may also be present.

Big Hill Springs Provincial Park has pit toilets. Gas and food can be obtained in Cochrane.

JOAN McDONALD

C-2 Grand Valley Road/Springbank Raptor Route

This scenic area provides the opportunity for observing the spring raptor migration close to the city. Although the Grand Valley/Horse Creek section is noted for large numbers of eagles in early spring, some raptors should be seen here at any season. The Springbank section is on gravel roads and offers less variety. These are suggested routes only. Most roads west of Cochrane will have some raptors at this season.

The **Grand Valley Road** portion of the route begins in Cochrane at the intersection of Hwy 1A and Hwy 22 (**km 0.0**). Hawks are often seen hovering at or soaring above the hills on the north side of the highway. Head west on Hwy 1A for 6.7 km to Grand Valley Road (marked by a green and white sign) and turn right. The route from this point is poorly paved and the roadway is narrow; some sections are being upgraded and may be gravel-surfaced. For the next nine winding kilometres, during the spring migration peak from mid-March to mid-April, Bald Eagles are especially common. In the early morning hours they may be seen on fenceposts or sitting on the ground, waiting for thermals to develop or for the prevailing westerly winds to begin. Large brown eagles may be either immature Bald or Golden Eagles. A scope is very helpful in determining age or species, since the birds are often 200 metres or more from the road. Rough-legged Hawks also are seen here in early April, so check any kettles of soaring birds for the distinctive flight silhouettes of eagles, buteos, falcons or ravens. Nest boxes along this route are likely to feature Tree Swallows rather than Mountain Bluebirds. The prominent ridge on the western side of this picturesque valley is known as the Wildcat Hills—it is private range land and is not accessible to the general public. A small gravel road, Wildcat Hills Road (11.9 km), crosses the ridge, however, and birding is possible from this.

The eagle migration coincides with the emergence of the male Richardson's Ground Squirrels. These energetic rodents have absolutely no fear of vehicles, especially while chasing rivals, and will often blindly race towards oncoming cars. It is essential that drivers DO NOT SWERVE to miss these apparently suicidal motions—you could

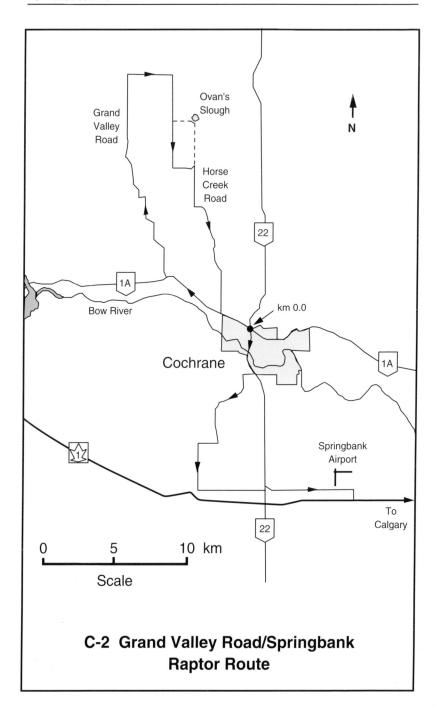

**C-2 Grand Valley Road/Springbank
Raptor Route**

endanger your passengers or other vehicles nearby. Their procreative abilities and inexplicable luck in avoiding most auto tires ensures the continuation of this species.

Northeast of the intersection with a gravel road from the east at 15.4 km, an exposed rock outcrop provides a well-used vantage point and perch for eagles and a favourable wind current for soaring raptors. Watch for coyotes in this area too, although they may be seen anywhere along the route. To the west is the meandering Grand Valley Creek, impeded at this point by a series of beaver dams. Few birds other than Canada Goose and Red-winged Blackbird can be found here after the waterfowl migration is over. This section of the route, particularly the hill topped by poplars at 20.7 km, has been the hunting range in irruptive winters for Northern Hawk Owl.

Turn right (east) at the next intersection (22 km). Watch for accipiters and American Kestrel along this section in summer and Northern Shrike in winter. Another turn to the right (25.3 km) will start the southbound portion of the trip. To the southeast is the gradually deepening and widening Horse Creek valley which you cross when you turn left (east) at 31.8 km. The road then heads south until Hwy 1A is reached. Compared to Grand Valley Road, more hawks but fewer eagles will be seen in the Horse Creek valley. Power poles should be scrutinized closely for such species as Prairie Falcon (uncommon) and Gyrfalcon (rare) in addition to the buteos.

OPTIONAL SECTION: In spring, if the roads are dry, you may turn east at 28.5 km onto a gravel road and up a fairly steep short hill. After 1.6 km a large pond (locally known as **Ovan's Slough**) is reached, on the north side of the road. Most waterfowl can be seen here, in addition to Common Snipe, Sora, and Yellow-headed Blackbird. Turn right at the slough and drive south for 3 km to rejoin the main route.

The **Springbank** portion of the route also begins at the junction of Hwy 1A and Hwy 22 (**km 0.0**). Head south on Hwy 22 and after crossing the Bow River watch for a road on the right at the top of the hill (3.5 km). Turn west here. At the T-intersection (4.4 km) turn left and head south along a winding road around Towers Ridge; bluebird nest boxes are numerous here. Turn right (west) at the first intersection (10.5 km) and then left at the paved road (11.9 km). To the west, the Copithorne Ridge may have small numbers of either eagle species during migration. At the crest of the steep hill prepare to make a left (east) turn, opposite a double row of spruce trees (15.1 km). There are natural hedges on both sides of the road for the next 5 km; American Tree Sparrow may occur here in late winter. These hedges can trap snow in drifts deep enough to stop any car—so avoid this section immediately after a severe storm. During migration, Bald Eagles are often seen sitting on fenceposts in this area. Turn left onto Hwy 22 (20 km), then after only 0.2 km turn right (east) onto the continuation of the gravel road parallelling the Trans-Canada Highway. The fields around Springbank Airport (26.8 km) attract Rough-legged Hawks throughout most winters. Turn south at 28.4 km for the Trans-Canada Highway and the return to the city. Eagles and hawks can often be seen from the highway in this area.

Gas and food are available in Cochrane.

ROSS DICKSON

C-3 The Water Valley Area

This area, which is undergoing rapid development, is located about 45 minutes driving time northwest of Calgary. From the east, aspen-covered rolling hills near Hwy 22 give way to the conifers and muskeg of the boreal foothills. In recent years seismic trails and logging roads have criss-crossed the entire area. Cheap grazing leases have lured farmers to exploit and expand the clearings, and many Calgarians have bought acreages to develop as weekend residences. This human influx has had a mixed effect on the local wildlife. Species such as Coyote, White-tailed Deer and American Crow which can benefit from additional forest "edge" are increasing, while local rarities such as the Connecticut Warbler suffer from the loss of habitat.

During summer this area hosts a variety of mountain and parkland species. Feeder watchers report Gray Jay, Blue Jay, Rose-breasted Grosbeak, Purple Finch, Pine Siskin and Evening Grosbeak. In the mature mixed forests are Northern Goshawk; Ruffed Grouse; both

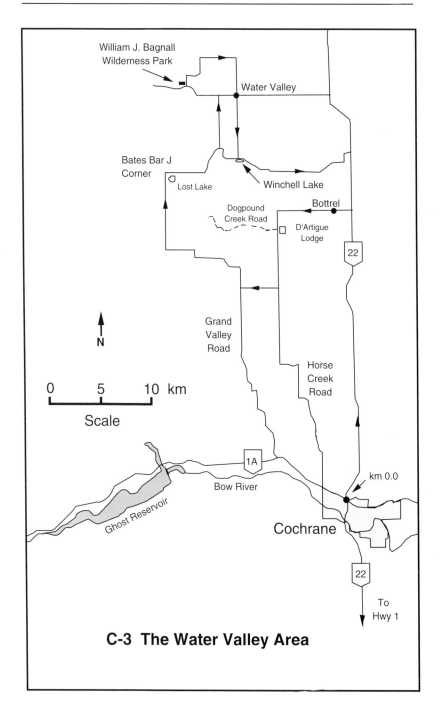

C-3 The Water Valley Area

Yellow-bellied and Red-naped Sapsuckers; Pileated Woodpecker; Swainson's and Hermit Thrushes; Solitary Vireo; Ovenbird; and Connecticut Warbler. Muskegs with beaver ponds support a variety of species such as Ring-necked Duck, Hooded Merganser (uncommon), Sora, Solitary Sandpiper, Alder Flycatcher and Wilson's Warbler.

What makes this area of particular interest to local birders however, are the owls in winter. The annual Christmas Bird Count centred on the Wildlife Reserve of Western Canada has listed a total of nine species of owl since 1974. Since the mid-1980s only Great Horned, Northern Pygmy-, Barred, Great Gray and Northern Saw-whet may be considered as widespread in their proper habitat, while Snowy, Northern Hawk, Short-eared and Boreal are apparently more subject to annual fluctuations.

Before heading into the foothills, birders unfamiliar with the area should take certain precautions. Elevations near Water Valley are higher than in Calgary, which means that it is colder and wetter. Many of the roads on this suggested route are gravel-surfaced and can become very slippery or muddy from the frequent snow or rain showers, or rutted from truck traffic. Spring breakup, which can occur anytime from late March to mid-May, may make certain sections impassable for passenger cars, although pickup trucks seldom have a problem with clearance. Some portions of the area are sparsely populated, but if you have obvious vehicle problems nearly all passersby will offer assistance. Roads are often narrow with limited visibility, so it is essential to pull well over to the right when making stops for birding. The area has an abundance of "No Trespassing" signs meant to discourage hunters. Birders are seldom refused walking access if permission is requested from landholders, but there are some exceptions—so ASK FIRST.

Essential requirements for successful owling:

- A reliable vehicle with good tire tread.
- A favourable weather forecast (wind, cloudy nights or precipitation are generally poor conditions for owling).
- Topographic map 82/O with a scale of 1:250,000 from Alberta Forestry, Lands and Wildlife (easier to read and more recently updated than federal maps).
- Ability to toot like a local Northern Pygmy-Owl. Unlike most

available recordings these local birds utter a single, not a double, note. Tapes are generally ineffective in this area—it is preferable to listen for spontaneous calls.

- Ability to be at the route before sunrise or in late afternoon for peak owl activity.
- Patience and a sense of humour. At best, for example, one trip in five in the likeliest habitat and at the most favourable time of day actually produces Great Gray Owl.

The following suggested main route covers a wide variety of habitats. It is designed to make use of the best maintained roads in the Water Valley area and to minimize travel on roads with only one exit. Any public road may lead to good owl habitat, but for safety reasons consult your map frequently when venturing off main routes. Logging or well access roads should not be considered public roads if they are posted with company signs. The map incorporates optional sections and short cuts for greater flexibility. For best results do not try the whole route at once. Owls tend to remain in the same general area, so ask around or phone the City's wildlife hotline for up-to–date information on sightings.

Head north on Hwy 22 from the 4-way intersection with Hwy 1A at Cochrane (**km 0.0**). In winter, watch fenceposts and power lines in this agricultural area for raptors such as Rough-legged Hawk, Gyrfalcon, Prairie Falcon, and Northern Hawk Owl. In summer, the most common species are Swainson's and Red-tailed Hawks and American Kestrel. Turn left (west) at the well-marked intersection for Bottrel (24.8 km) and drive 6.5 km to the stop sign at Horse Creek Road. Turn left again and head south 1.7 km to an intersection, marked on the east side of the road by the D'Artigue Community Hall (33 km in total).

OPTIONAL SECTION: It can be worthwhile turning west here onto the winding road along **Dogpound Creek**, taking the left fork after about 3 km and continuing for another 2 km. This is a very narrow gravel road with many small hills and it will be necessary to retrace your steps to D'Artigue. Any type of forest owl is possible in the Dogpound Creek watershed, and they are just as likely to be perched on fenceposts as on trees. In summer the brushy area along the creek is good habitat for warblers such as Northern Waterthrush.

From D'Artigue continue south for 4.8 km to a paved intersection, then turn right (west) past the fenced Wildlife Reserve of Western Canada. This is a non-profit organization which raises Swift Foxes for release into the wild—it is not open to the public. Accipiters may occasionally be seen along this section. Immediately west of the WRWC the tree-covered hill to the south of the road has been the winter home of a Northern Hawk Owl in irruptive years. Sharp-tailed Grouse and Northern Shrike are occasionally seen in the fields surrounding the Reserve. Both Bald and Golden Eagles may be seen during spring migration. At the next stop sign (41.1 km), turn right (north) onto a paved road. This is the northern extension of Grand Valley Road. (See route C-2. By using this approach to the area, the afternoon could be spent watching for diurnal raptors and the evening looking for owls). A series of west and north turns through thick coniferous forest results in a northwesterly direction over a distance of 9.5 km. Eventually you will emerge briefly from the trees into a large pastured area. Northern Shrike may occur here in winter. Back into the trees, the road continues north. The edges of large clearcut openings in the forest here, together with the scattered poplar trees within them, are good places to look for owls at dawn and dusk. Crossbills may also be present if there is an abundant cone crop.

At the corner marked by signs for the Bates Bar J Ranch, turn right (east), through a Texas gate (60 km). The road now trends in a northeasterly direction. Both large and small owls, Pileated Woodpecker, and the locally uncommon Red Crossbill have all been recorded in this section, so many stops are advisable. At the intersection with Winchell Lake Road (63.2 km) turn left and head north for 4.3 km to a paved road (S.R. 579). Turn left (west) for 3.2 km, then turn right (north), immediately after crossing the Little Red Deer River (70.9 km).

OPTIONAL SECTION: **William J. Bagnall Wilderness Park** (Formerly Silver Creek Park) This municipal campground (fee charged in summer for day-use) is located 1.5 km to the west of the main route. Western Flycatcher breeds here and it can be good for warblers in late May and June. Nashville Warbler and Black-throated Blue Warbler, rare spring vagrants in the Region, were recorded here in June 1986. In winter, if the access road has been snowplowed, it may be worth a brief visit.

Continuing on the main route the road follows the Little Red Deer River northeast, then along a straight north portion through some more good Barred and Great Gray Owl habitat to a stop sign at a paved road, known locally as Big Prairie Road (77.2 km). Turn right and continue for 1.3 km to a large marshy area. This has occasionally attracted a pair of Sandhill Cranes in recent summers. This type of habitat can be found between many of the treed ridges throughout the area. About 2 km beyond the marsh turn right (south); the hamlet of Water Valley will be reached after about 3 km (87 km). Winter feeders here attract both Gray and Blue Jays, Mountain and Boreal Chick-adees, and Evening Grosbeak.

From Water Valley continue south for a further 5.2 km to a T-intersection. Turn left (east) for the return to Hwy 22. In this section Northern Pygmy-Owl has been reported from the **Winchell Lake** area. Beaver dams have created a series of ponds and marshes which are home in spring and summer to Ring-necked Duck and infrequently, Hooded Merganser. Sandhill Cranes have been reported occasionally. In winter, watch for both Barred and Great Gray Owls near the intersection with Horse Creek Road, 2.6 km from the Winchell Lake corner.

Gas and meals can be obtained in Water Valley.

ROSS DICKSON

C-4 The Forestry Trunk Road

This driving route takes the birder from relatively open country into heavily forested rugged foothills. It is excellent for migrating raptors as well as foothills specialties such as Northern Pygmy-Owl and Rosy Finch. The route is most rewarding during March-April and again in October-November. Snowfall can be heavy in this area well into spring and early in the fall, so undertake this drive with some caution. The distance one way to Water Valley from the junction with Hwy 1A is 90 km. Allow two hours plus to drive this, depending on what birds are encountered and how much time is spent on side trips.

The route begins (**km 0.0**) at the junction of Hwy 1A and the Forestry Trunk Road (S.R. 940), approximately 12.5 km west of the Hwy 22

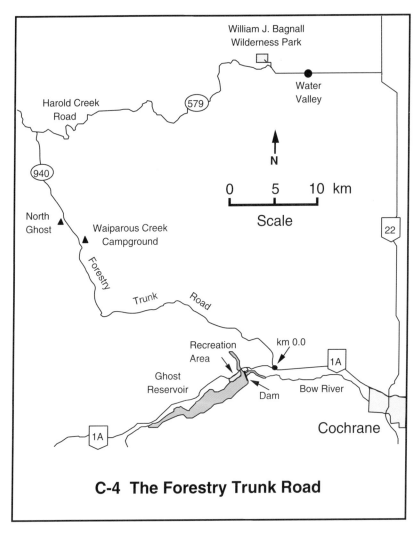

C-4 The Forestry Trunk Road

intersection in Cochrane. Turn right (north). The first 30 km are paved but the road is narrow, twisting and rough in places; from then on to the Harold Creek turnoff it is a good gravel road. After 1.5 km Beaupre Lake will be seen on the left, behind the gas well (Caution: do not cross the fence here). This small foothills pond is shallow and can be dry but usually provides a resting spot for migrating waterfowl, especially in spring. Wood Duck and Eurasian Wigeon have been seen here in April and Trumpeter Swan in April-May. From this point through to the bridge over Waiparous Creek (17.0 km) watch for migrant raptors. Golden Eagle nests in the area and Northern Hawk Owl is a possibility from November through to April. At the Waiparous Creek bridge check for American Dipper and listen for Northern Pygmy-Owl. The road enters the Forest Reserve at 27.1 km. Watch for Bohemian Waxwing, Snow Bunting, Rosy Finch and both crossbill species from this point right through to Water Valley. Another bridge over Waiparous Creek occurs at 37.2 km. Again check the creek for American Dipper. Northern Pygmy-Owl can be almost anywhere on this route, so whenever possible listen for its distinctive tooting.

The **North Ghost Recreation Area** has two campgrounds. The first, Waiparous Creek, is reached at 35.3 km. The second, North Ghost, is on the left at 39.4 km. This campground is closed between October 8th and May 21st each year but it can be birded by walking in (check the snow depth before parking off the highway). The spruce woods should yield Spruce Grouse. Summer residents include Olive-sided, Dusky and Western Flycatchers; Swainson's and Varied Thrushes; Ruby-crowned Kinglet; and Yellow-rumped Warbler. In spring, more open ridge tops in this general area may harbour small numbers of Blue Grouse. The Waiparous Valley viewpoint occurs at 42 km. A breathtaking view of peaks of the Front Range of the Rocky Mountains can be enjoyed here. The Harold Creek/Salisbury Road junction is reached at 46 km. Turn right (east) here. This gravel road can have bad sections, especially during the spring thaw—so undertake this part of the route with caution. Most of the birds discussed above are possible along this stretch as well. Additionally, be on the lookout for Great Gray Owl. The road leaves the Forest Reserve at 65.5 km and the foothills community of Water Valley appears at 87 km, about 5 km beyond the bridge over the Little Red Deer River. 10 km east of Water Valley is Hwy 22; turn south for a direct route back to Hwy 1A.

Gas and meals can be obtained in Water Valley. For a taste of western hospitality try the Water Valley Saloon.

OPTIONAL SECTION: **Ghost Reservoir** is a large, deep waterbody formed by the damming of the Bow immediately downstream of its confluence with the Ghost River. Large numbers of waterfowl, grebes and loons gather here during spring and fall migration. Depending on how much time you have at your disposal and the time of year, you may wish to visit this location before starting the route. There are two access points at the eastern end. From the junction with the Forestry Trunk Road you can either drive 2.8 km west to a minor gravel road on the left. Turn here and continue until the road divides. Keep to the right and park near the dam. This vantage point offers a good view of the Ghost River as it enters the reservoir. Or you can drive 4.5 km west from the Forestry Trunk Road junction to a small recreation area on the shoreline. Pacific Loon has been seen in the vicinity of the bridge in late October-early November. Other species to watch for at this time include Oldsquaw, White-winged Scoter and Surf Scoter.

DOUG COLLISTER

C-5 The Sheep River Valley

This route begins in flat farmlands on the south side of Calgary and ends 85 km southwest of the city, just inside the Front Range of the Rocky Mountains. The route travelled includes flat farmland, gently rolling grassland, aspen parkland, river bottoms, mixed woods of the foothills and coniferous forest of the mountains. The round trip of 170 km takes about three hours (1.5 hours one way) if one doesn't stop. However, the main focus of this trip is a full day that can be spent in the **Sheep River Wildlife Sanctuary**, approximately one hour from Calgary. During spring (March-April) and fall (September-October) this particular area can produce raptor migrations that are the best known for Alberta. Data generated since 1983 has shown that daily totals of over 600 raptors of 17 species are possible, but numbers are more likely to be in the 50–150 range.

From Calgary to the Sanctuary many species typical of southern Alberta can be seen during summer, such as Swainson's Hawk, American Kestrel, Mourning Dove, Northern Flicker (Red-shafted, Yellow-shafted and hybrid forms are all possible in southern Alberta), Mountain Bluebird, Cedar Waxwing, Red-eyed Vireo, Yellow Warbler, Clay-colored Sparrow, Vesper Sparrow and Western Meadowlark. From the Sanctuary west to the mountains typical summer species are Ruffed Grouse, Red-naped Sapsucker, Hairy Woodpecker, Dusky Fly-catcher, Western Flycatcher, Gray Jay, Mountain Chickadee, Townsend's

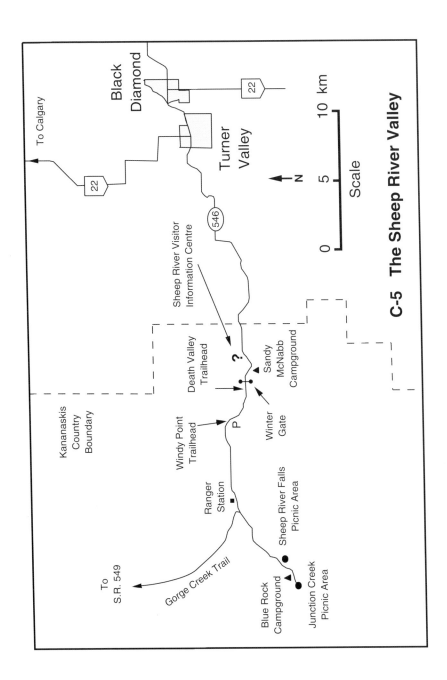

To Calgary

Black Diamond

22

Turner Valley

22

Sheep River Visitor Information Centre

546

N

Death Valley Trailhead

?

Sandy McNabb Campground

Kananaskis Country Boundary

Windy Point Trailhead

P

Winter Gate

Ranger Station

To S.R. 549

Gorge Creek Trail

Sheep River Falls Picnic Area

Blue Rock Campground

Junction Creek Picnic Area

Scale

0   5   10 km

C-5   The Sheep River Valley

Solitaire, Tennessee Warbler, Yellow-rumped (Audubon's) Warbler, Western Tanager, Chipping Sparrow, Dark-eyed Junco and Pine Siskin.

The starting point (**km 0.0**) is the southern edge of Calgary where Hwy 2 intersects with Hwy 22X (the Marquis of Lorne Trail). At this intersection turn right (west) onto Hwy 22X. For the next 18 km the highway passes through an area of farmland interspersed with some aspen clumps and seasonal ponds. During spring and fall many migrant raptors can be observed in this area. Wherever seasonal ponds occur watch for swans; with rare exception, small parties of swans in this area during migration are Trumpeters.

After driving for 18 km the intersection of roads to Bragg Creek (Hwy 22 West) and Turner Valley (Hwy 22 South) is reached. Turn left and continue south to the town of Turner Valley. For the next 27 km the highway winds back and forth through ranchland/farmland with more extensive clumps of aspen and willow. Again, during spring and fall, watch for migrant raptors and Trumpeter Swans. Both Bald and Golden Eagles are more frequently seen in this area (particularly in March and April). If you stop along this section of highway take care as the road is narrow, undivided and has a lot of traffic.

After reaching the northern edge of the town of Turner Valley, drive a further kilometre to a four way stop in the downtown area (46 km). Turn right (west) onto S.R. 546. Five blocks further on the road takes a turn to the north at the western edge of town. Follow the signs directing you to the Sandy McNabb and Bluerock Recreation Areas. For the next 15 km the road winds mainly west through ranchland with increasingly extensive areas of aspen and mixed woods. During migration, raptors of all species are frequently seen. On occasion, especially in late summer, Great Gray Owls have occurred along this section of road. From early spring to late fall, Mountain Bluebirds are almost always seen. During migration (particularly in early October) up to five Northern Shrikes can be seen in a single day.

The Kananaskis Country boundary is reached at 61 km. For the next 2 km the road parallels a creek valley with numerous beaver ponds. The mixed woods in this area can be very good for late spring/early summer birding. Yellow-bellied Flycatcher and Solitary Vireo have occasionally been found here at this season. In late fall and early winter Northern Pygmy-Owls have been seen along the road.

The Sandy McNabb Campground is reached at 66 km. Red-naped Sap-sucker and Pileated Woodpecker are frequently found in this area of spruce/pine and mixed woods. An easy hiking trail north through **Death Valley** starts here. Ruffed Grouse occur, and with some effort, Spruce Grouse can be found in late spring and early summer. Death Valley can be productive in early summer because of its extensive beaver ponds and areas of mixed woods. For those with time to spare, several hours can be profitably used hiking up this valley. For the main trip however, continue west past the Sandy McNabb Campground. From this point on the road is closed to vehicles between December 1 and May 15 each year. Anywhere along this section of road (particular-ly south to the river valley) can be productive for birding.

After passing the eastern boundary (with large sign) of the Sheep River Wildlife Sanctuary the **Windy Point** parking lot is reached at 69.1 km, on the west side of the road. From this spot one can observe an extensive raptor migration in the spring and fall. Every species of diurnal raptor that occurs in Alberta has been recorded here. Literally hundreds of raptors have been seen in a single day, including Osprey, Bald Eagle, Sharp-shinned and Cooper's Hawks, Northern Goshawk, Harlan's (ssp.) Hawk, Golden Eagle and Peregrine Falcon. Prairie Falcon breeds in the area. The last week of March and the first week of April, and the last two weeks of September and the first week of October can be particularly rewarding. However, even at the height of migration there can be days with almost zero raptor movement. A hiking trail leads north from the parking area through a valley between two high ridges. About 1.5 km north on this steeper trail is a junction marked by a large trail sign. The trail to the east climbs to the top of the ridge (another 0.5 km). Along this ridge-top hooting male Blue Grouse can be found in May. Black-capped, Mountain and Boreal Chickadees are permanent residents in this general area. In fall, main-ly after mountain snowstorms, hundreds of Rosy Finches can be seen. Careful searching will usually reveal a few individuals of the Hep-burn's subspecies.

Continuing the drive the Sheep River Ranger Station is reached at 75.2 km. Many Bighorn Sheep spend the entire year here and, partic-ularly in late fall (rutting season), the sheep are very tame and can be observed easily. This area of open grassland, bordered on the north by cliffs, also produces an excellent raptor migration. The Gorge Creek Trail heads north at 75.4 km; for this trip continue west along the main road. The highway crosses Gorge Creek at 76 km; from here to the end of the road (another 8 km) the terrain becomes increasingly more mountainous, with mainly a coniferous forest cover.

The western boundary of the Sheep River Wildlife Sanctuary is reached at 81.5 km. At the **Sheep River Falls Picnic Area** (or wherever the river comes close to the road) one can stop in summer and search for breeding Harlequin Duck, Western Flycatcher, American Dipper and Townsend's Solitaire. Northern Hawk Owl and Black-backed Woodpecker are permanent residents of the area, although they are infrequently observed.

The Bluerock Campground is reached at 82.6 km. Of the two campgrounds, this is probably the best one for a birder to stay at. The Sheep River Trail ends at the **Junction Creek Picnic Area** after a further 1.4 km. During the summer, many breeding montane birds can be seen in this general area. These include Spruce Grouse; Three-toed Woodpecker; Olive-sided and Dusky Flycatchers; Gray Jay; Mountain Chickadee; Brown Creeper; Golden-crowned Kinglet; Townsend's Solitaire; Swainson's, Hermit and Varied Thrushes; Yellow-rumped (Audubon's) Warbler; Northern Waterthrush; MacGillivray's Warbler; Western Tanager; and Pine Grosbeak. Steller's Jay and Clark's Nutcracker have also been seen in the area on an irregular basis.

Map Those birders unfamiliar with the area should stop at the Sheep River Visitor Information Centre, on the right-hand side of the road, just prior to the Sandy McNabb Campground. An excellent topographic map of the area, showing the hiking trails, can be obtained here.

Gas, food and accommodation are available in Turner Valley.

WAYNE W. SMITH

C-6 Brown-Lowery Recreation Area

Brown-Lowery Recreation Area is located in the foothills, less than 40 km southwest of Calgary. It consists of 278 ha of mature woodland. White Spruce is the dominant species of tree, with pockets of aspen in places; small creeks and marshy areas occur between the slopes. Birds found within Brown-Lowery are typical of the coniferous forest; a calm morning in winter may offer the best conditions for finding some of the more sought after species. Although birds are not numerous at any time of year, the scenery alone is worth the effort. At least half a day is needed to bird Brown-Lowery thoroughly.

Directions are given as an 87 km driving loop which can be modified, depending on weather conditions and the season. Forest birds can be notoriously difficult to find in windy weather—so check the weather forecast before setting out as this area is in the chinook belt, where strong winds can occur at any time of year. The route begins at the southern edge of the city where Macleod Trail (Hwy 2) intersects with Hwy 22X (the Marquis of Lorne Trail) (**km 0.0**). Head west on Hwy 22X for about 18 km, then watch for the Hwy 22 sign for Turner Valley and Black Diamond. Turn left (south) on Hwy 22 and continue for 6.5 km before turning right onto Plummer's Road (gravel-surfaced; may be muddy and rutted after prolonged rain). After 3.3 km, turn left at a T-intersection (240 St W) and follow this winding road for another 8 km, first south then towards the west. Brown-Lowery Recreation Area is located on the left (south) side of the road—watch for small yellow signs on the fence reading "Provincial Recreation Area Boundary" and a parking lot among the conifers, entered via Texas gates (36 km). In winter, park on the roadside rather than in the unplowed parking area.

The majority of birds found here can be seen throughout the park, not just in one particular area. The trail system consists of footpaths, cut-lines and an old logging road. The terrain is hilly, but walking is not difficult. It is easy to get lost in here however, as directional signs are sparse—so be careful to know where you are.

In winter, this is one of the best places in the Calgary area to look for Three-toed and Black-backed Woodpeckers. Both are scarce however, and more than one visit may be necessary to see either species. Your

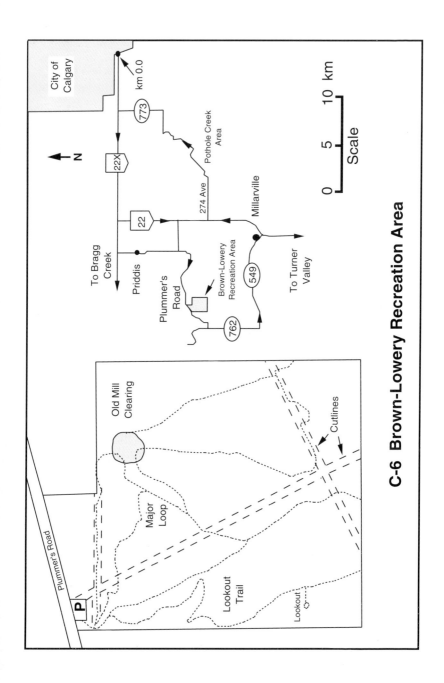

C-6 Brown-Lowery Recreation Area

best bet is to bird areas where there are dead or dying spruce trees. Downy, Hairy and Pileated Woodpeckers are all uncommon residents in areas of mixed woodland. Red-naped Sapsucker is an uncommon summer resident.

Gray Jay and Boreal Chickadee are common residents. They can be found throughout the park with relative ease, except at the height of the breeding season when they become very secretive. Red-breasted Nuthatch is a scarce winter resident and uncommon summer breeder. White-breasted Nuthatch is a scarce winter resident; look for it in the mixed woodland around the old mill. Brown Creeper is a scarce winter resident of the spruce forest. Both species of kinglet occur: Ruby-crowned is a common breeding bird and Golden-crowned is uncommon in the spruce trees in winter.

In spring and summer listen and watch for Veery, Swainson's, Hermit and Varied Thrushes; Solitary Vireo; and Tennessee, Yellow-rumped (both "Audubon's" and "Myrtle" nest in this area) and Townsend's Warblers. Cape May Warbler is a rare summer resident in this part of the province; it was first recorded at Brown-Lowery in 1982 and should be looked for.

Bohemian Waxwing, Pine Grosbeak, White-winged Crossbill and Evening Grosbeak are all erratic winter visitors to the park. Pine Siskins are common in summer, but very rare in winter.

Barred, Great Gray, Boreal and Northern Saw-whet Owls have been confirmed as nesting. Your chances of seeing the first three species are slim however, as they are very secretive. Usually they are only seen when flushed or while being mobbed by other birds. Northern Saw-whet Owls are most easily found at night when they are calling. Northern Goshawk is an uncommon year-round resident. Cooper's Hawk nests in the park; it can sometimes be found along the forest edge, hunting for small birds.

There are pit toilets adjacent to the parking area. Gas can be obtained in Millarville.

If time permits in spring and summer, you may wish to extend the route to cover some entirely different habitats. In this case, continue southwest from the parking lot to S.R. 762 (39 km). (This is also the

connector road to Bragg Creek and the Elbow River valley.)   Northern
Hawk Owl has been observed near this intersection in winter.   Turn
left and head south, then left again (44.7 km) onto S.R. 549 which joins
Hwy 22 at Millarville.   Watch for waterfowl in the creeks visible from
the road, and for raptors perched in the trees.   In early spring, this is
on the migration route for Trumpeter Swan, Bald Eagle and Rough-
legged Hawk.   Turn left (north) onto Hwy 22 (55.5 km) and at the sign-
post for the Leighton Centre (62 km, about 8 km from Millarville), turn
right onto a gravel road (274 Ave W).   (In winter, or if the road is wet,
it may be wise to continue north on Hwy 22 to Calgary).   This 19 km-
long winding section of the route, through scenic ranching country,
becomes S.R. 773 and rejoins Hwy 22X close to the city.   Good views of
the potholes and marshes along Pothole Creek can be obtained.
Species to watch for in spring include Ring-necked Duck, Barrow's
Goldeneye and Bufflehead.   Summer residents include Red-necked
Grebe, Eared Grebe and Black Tern.   Rough-legged Hawk may be
common in winter; Prairie Falcon and Gyrfalcon (rare) may also occur.

MICHAEL HARRISON

C-7 Bow Valley Provincial Park

Bow Valley Provincial Park is located on the Trans-Canada Highway
immediately east of the Front Range of the Rocky Mountains.   Here,
the intersection of montane, foothills and grassland environments
creates a diversity of habitats.   More than 140 species of birds have
been identified within the park.   A potentially excellent location for
uncommon warblers (especially during migration), it is also the closest
location to Calgary where Calliope Hummingbird occurs regularly.
The best months for birding are May and June.   A full day is required
to cover the major habitat types; alternatively, either of the park's two
campgrounds can be used as a base for visiting nearby birding locali-
ties.   From Calgary a birder has the choice of two routes.   The quickest
and most direct is to take the Trans-Canada Highway (Hwy 1) west to
the interchange with Hwy 1X, a distance of 65 km from Canada
Olympic Park.   Access to Bow Valley Provincial Park is from Hwy 1X
and is well sign-posted.   A slower but perhaps more scenic route is to

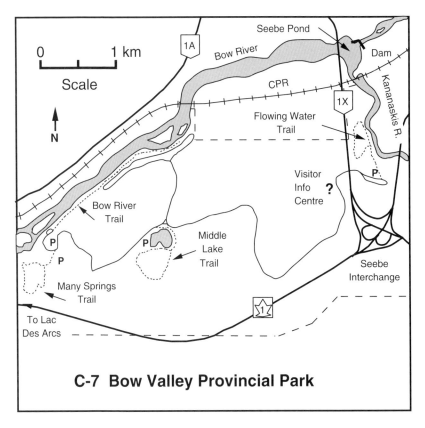

C-7 Bow Valley Provincial Park

take Hwy 1A, the extension of Crowchild Trail in the northwest part of the city. In this case turn left (south) onto Hwy 1X and drive 3.3 km to the park entrance.

The Trans-Canada Highway divides the park into an eastern and a western block. All the birding locations discussed here are in the developed western block. This western block is cut in two by Hwy 1X, with the Bow River forming the park boundary to the north-west, and the Kananaskis River to the northeast. A special aspect is the variation in vegetation from one end of the park to the other. There are extensive grasslands to the east, mixed woodlands of Aspen and White Spruce, and large areas dominated by Lodgepole Pine with small pockets of Douglas Fir and Limber Pine. Aquatic habitats are well-represented with beaver ponds, freshwater springs, small lakes and river communities.

Four hiking trails provide access to the park's major birding areas. Probably the most interesting is the **Flowing Water Trail** which starts from the Willow Rock Campground on the eastern side of Hwy 1X. This area is best visited early in the morning when the birds are most active and the campers still torpid. From Hwy 1X drive through the registration area and park by the washrooms. Watch for Rufous Hummingbird (June-July) at the small, planted shrubbery around the buildings. The open grassland of the campground is a good area for Western Meadowlark, Mountain Bluebird, and Savannah, Vesper and Clay-colored Sparrows. Just north of the washrooms is a small trail that winds through the wooded area of the campground to the start of the Flowing Water Trail. This section may produce Three-toed Woodpecker (uncommon); Black-capped, Mountain and Boreal Chickadees; Brown Creeper; Ruby-crowned Kinglet; and Swainson's Thrush. In winter the small, spring-fed stream stays open and Common Snipe and American Dipper can occasionally be found. Finches, such as White-winged Crossbill, Common Redpoll and Evening Grosbeak are possibilities in the crowns of the conifers.

Once through the campground you arrive at the Flowing Water loop trail. Keep to the right and you will soon be walking along the banks of the Kananaskis River. Watch for Bald Eagle, Spotted Sandpiper, American Dipper and Townsend's Solitaire along this stretch. Continue until an open hillside is reached; here an Eastern Phoebe can often be seen sitting on an exposed Douglas Fir branch. At the top of the hill look for soaring hawks, Osprey, Common Raven and occasionally, eagles. Rufous Hummingbirds are common hereabouts in June and July, and Calliope has been seen. Continue along the pathway until it descends into a dense stand of Aspen Poplar. Typical birds in this area include Least Flycatcher, Warbling Vireo and Yellow Warbler. Unusual species of warblers have also been seen: a single male Chestnut-sided Warbler sang on territory here in 1987, 1988 and 1990. After this area of dense woodland, one of the best beaver dams of the park and a most interesting area for birds, is reached. Species found here include Barrow's Goldeneye; Sora (listen in spring, there is nearly always one calling); Common Snipe; Western Wood-Pewee; Alder (vree-feel) and Willow (FITZ-bew) Flycatchers; Northern Waterthrush; Common Yellowthroat; and American Goldfinch. Unfortunately, the Alder and Willow Flycatchers occur in the same habitat so identification requires familiarity with their songs. The willows between the trail and the highway can also be good for migrating warblers; in fall

Rusty Blackbird can often be found. The final part of the trail leads through an area of dense willow bush. In June this is probably one of the best areas within the park for locating Calliope Hummingbird; check the tips of dead trees for these little jewels. Ovenbird can often be heard calling in this area.

From the Willow Rock Campground, drive west across Hwy 1X and enter the main part of the park. Continue on this road until Middle Lake is reached. The picnic area and interpretive trail can be good for Ruffed Grouse, Mountain Bluebird, Yellow-rumped Warbler and Dark-eyed Junco. Common and Barrow's Goldeneyes, Ring-necked Duck and Killdeer may be seen at the lake. A large herd of Elk often use this area. In winter the road is kept open to here. If time is limited, continue beyond Middle Lake and take the left-hand fork to the Many Springs Parking Lot.

The **Many Springs area and loop trail** can be very productive. Watch the trees for both Willow and Dusky Flycatchers, Yellow-rumped Warbler, Dark-eyed Junco and Pine Siskin. The area's abundance of flowers seems to attract large numbers of Rufous Hummingbirds, each tall snag sporting a territorial male. Along the far side of the lake you should find Common Yellowthroat and Wilson's Warbler. Nashville (May-June) and other unusual warblers are reported here quite often. In fall this is an excellent location for migrants. Mixed feeding flocks are typical, so let the chickadees lead you to the warblers.

Finally, the Bow River Trail also offers access to good birding areas. From Many Springs continue downhill and park at the Whitefish Picnic Area. The trail winds along the Bow River for 2.5 km through a variety of shrubby and woodland habitats. As this area is heavily used, it is best birded early in the morning or in the evening. Watch the river for Violet-green Swallow, Belted Kingfisher and Osprey. Although the park is well to the west of the major shorebird migration routes, interesting species can sometimes be seen along the muddy shoreline, particularly in fall. At this time too, watch for migrant warblers and sparrows.

Elk, deer and beaver are the mammals most likely to be seen within the park; Black Bears are seen occasionally. An attempt has been made to reintroduce River Otters and released animals have been reported along the Kananaskis River. Numerous uncommon or unusual flowers, especially orchids, occur within the park; the Many Springs area is a good place to look for these in June. If you visit Bow Valley in spring or early summer be sure to have plenty of insect repellent, as mosquitoes and ticks easily outnumber the birds.

Seebe Pond Although it is outside the park boundary, another good birding location is the deep pond formed in the Bow River by the hydroelectric dam at Seebe. In early spring this is an excellent area for Common Loon and many species of waterfowl. In summer all six swallow species can be found at the dam; and in October and early November the deep water here is probably one of the most reliable locations for Surf Scoter in the Calgary area. American Dipper is regular below the dam. In late fall, all loons at the pond and upstream of the bridge should be scrutinized carefully.

Gas and groceries can be obtained at Exshaw; full tourist facilities are available in the town of Canmore.

DAVE ELPHINSTONE

C-8 Lac Des Arcs

Lac Des Arcs is a large, shallow lake adjacent to the Trans-Canada Highway within the Front Range of the Rocky Mountains, on the Bow River just west of Bow Valley Provincial Park. Despite the presence of a large cement works and the resulting degradation of the environment, it nevertheless is an important staging area for waterfowl and gulls in spring and fall, and is worth a stop on the way to Banff. During migration large numbers of Tundra Swans and surface-feeding ducks may be seen, together with smaller numbers of diving ducks such as Common Goldeneye, Bufflehead and Hooded Merganser. American Wigeon can be particularly abundant and these should be checked for the occasional Eurasian Wigeon, which has been recorded here in fall. Other rarities recorded here have been Parasitic Jaeger (two on Sept. 12, 1982) and Glaucous Gull (Nov. 2, 1985). Osprey and Bald Eagle are regularly seen.

The first access point is reached by driving west on the Trans-Canada Highway (Hwy 1) for about 8 km from the Seebe Interchange (Hwy 1X), then exiting to the right onto the access road to the Lac Des Arcs Campground. The eastern end of the lake can be scoped from the canoe launching area or from a vacant campsite. The Trans-Canada Highway parallels the southern shore of the lake, with three vehicle pull-outs offering further viewing opportunities. These occur at 0.6 km, 0.9 km, and l.6 km from the campground exit.

JOAN McDONALD

C-9 Smith Dorrien/Spray Trail

The Smith-Dorrien/Spray Trail (gravel-surfaced and rather dusty) stretches between the town of Canmore and Peter Lougheed Provincial Park, a distance of approximately 62 km. It allows access to a vast area containing coniferous forest, muskeg, subalpine and alpine habitats. Late spring through summer birding should produce species such as Spruce Grouse, Brewer's Sparrow and Townsend's Solitaire. A full day is required to cover all the sites in the area.

The fastest access is from downtown Canmore, where you follow the well-posted signs (white letters on brown or a white skier on brown) for the NORDIC CENTRE. While driving up, watch for Bighorn Sheep on the road and the fantastic scenery down below.

1.1 km past the entrance to the Nordic Centre is the turn-off to **Grassi Lakes** where there is a breeding colony of Violet-green Swallows. Turn left at the sign for the Grassi Lakes Recreation Area and drive 0.5 km to the parking lot. From this point there is a walk of about 1.5 km up to the lakes. You can choose between the hiking trail (marked) which is fairly steep but gives good views and the old power-line access road, which is less steep but has limited views. Grassi Lakes is a very attractive spot, where a cliff, pock-marked with caves, overlooks two small, algae-coloured lakes. The nesting colony of Violet-green Swallows on the cliff is large and spectacular. Other birds which may be found are Western Flycatcher, American Dipper, Swainson's Thrush and Yellow-rumped Warbler.

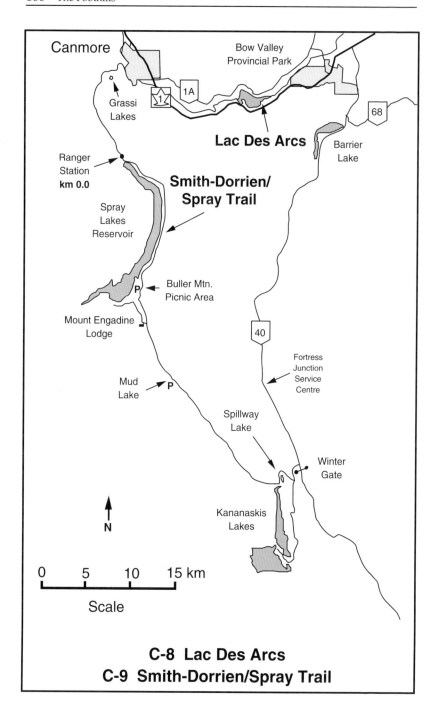

C-8 Lac Des Arcs
C-9 Smith-Dorrien/Spray Trail

Spray Lakes Reservoir is approximately 18 km from the centre of
Canmore, roughly 2 hours driving time from Calgary. A free campground is located to the west of the reservoir, accessed by the (rough)
public road over the dam at the northern end. Drinking water and
maps are available at the Ranger Station, 0.2 km north of the dam.

Distances will be given from the Ranger Station, so set your trip-meter
here (**km 0.0**). While driving south along the eastern shore, watch for
Osprey fishing near the dam. Common Loon, Common Goldeneye
and Common Merganser are also regular sights on the reservoir
(which is said to be good for Lake Trout fishing).

After driving 14.1 km south from the Ranger Station, park in the small
pull-out on the right-hand side of the road. About 50 m beyond the
parking area, on the left-hand side of the road, is a rather narrow
(about 60 m wide) avalanche area, cutting through the forest. It stretches all the way up to an alpine meadow on the flank of Mount Buller.
There is no man-made trail, but hiking up the 30° slope is not too difficult. Townsend's Solitaire and Hermit Thrush nest in the trees bordering the avalanche area (not dangerous in summer) you are climbing.
Bohemian Waxwing, White-crowned Sparrow and White-winged
Crossbill are also seen here. If you continue the ascent past the tree
line, listen for the calls and song of Brewer's Sparrow—the alpine race
of the species nests here. As you climb watch for a pair of Golden
Eagles which sometimes can be seen gliding over the area. Flocks of
Rosy Finches may occur in late summer and fall. Depending on the
amount of time you want to spend searching the woods bordering the
avalanche area, this climb could take anywhere from 1 1/2 to 4 hours;
carry warm clothing as it can be cool and windy above the tree line.

Continue driving south and park in the first parking lot at the **Buller
Mountain Picnic Area** (18.5 km). A short distance south of the parking lot lies a pond bordering the highway. Birding around the pond
should yield Solitary Sandpiper (nesting in the trees close to the
water), Olive-sided Flycatcher and Varied Thrush. Swainson's Thrush
can often be heard singing across the road in the shrubs and the first
trees of the slope. A half-hour walk along the trail which begins at the
western end of the first parking lot will usually add Yellow-rumped
(Audubon's) and Townsend's Warblers, Chipping Sparrow, Dark-eyed
(Oregon) Junco, and Pine Siskin to your list.

After leaving the Buller Mountain Picnic Area, drive a further 3.5 km and then turn right (west) onto the **Mount Engadine Lodge** access road (22.3 km). Park on the right, just before the bridge. Walk across this bridge and bird along the road as it passes beside the muskeg basin. You should see Yellow-rumped and Wilson's Warblers; Chipping, Lincoln's and White-crowned Sparrows; and Pine Siskin. As the road turns around the end of the muskeg and up the hill, Varied Thrush, "Oregon" Junco and White-winged Crossbill may be seen. Keep walking to the top (about 1 km from the bridge). A short distance further on, to your right, is one of the most interesting areas of the region. Slightly downslope from the road lies a re-growth area, now green with grass and low shrubs, and many old dead trees. Northern Flicker, Olive-sided Flycatcher, Mountain Bluebird and Townsend's Solitaire nest here, and Clark's Nutcracker is a frequent visitor. Some time spent walking the perimeter of this re-growth area and the surrounding woodland might yield Spruce Grouse. Three-toed and Black-backed Woodpeckers are also possible. In winter, feeders at Mount Engadine Lodge can be good for Steller's Jay.

Continuing your drive, the Chester Lake/Burstall Lakes trailheads are reached at 29 km. **Mud Lake** is immediately north of the junction. Bird around the lake and along the west shore of the creek flowing north from Mud Lake; this western shore can be reached by an unofficial footbridge, about 150 m north of the lake. You should be rewarded with Downy and Hairy Woodpeckers; Gray Jay; Common Raven; both species of waxwings; Common Yellowthroat; Chipping, Lincoln's, White-throated and White-crowned Sparrows; and with a bit of luck, a Red-naped Sapsucker.

About 2.5 km before Smith-Dorrien/Spray Trail ends at the junction with Kananaskis Lakes Trail, Spillway Lake can be seen on the right-hand side of the highway. This can be good for Common Loon, Ring-necked Duck, Barrow's Goldeneye, Osprey and Spotted Sandpiper.

As an alternative to retracing the route to Canmore, the drive may be continued on through Peter Lougheed Provincial Park (see route C-11) until Hwy 40 (Kananaskis Trail) is reached. This highway provides access north through the Kananaskis Valley to the Trans-Canada Highway or south over the Highwood Pass (see route C-12).

Meals can be obtained at Mount Engadine Lodge. Gas and snack foods are available at the Fortress Junction Service Centre (on Hwy 40). Full tourist facilities are available in Canmore.

LOUIS M. GUILLEMETTE

C-10 Sibbald Creek Trail

This 37 kilometre route within the foothills ecological region offers year-round birding, highlighted by the opportunity to hear (and occasionally see) five species of locally uncommon owls on late winter evenings. During spring and summer, about fifty species of birds may be found by stopping at marshes and hiking near picnic areas. This route is frequently exposed to strong winds—60 to 100 km/h gusts are common during Chinooks—so it is essential to know the weather forecast for the foothills before setting out, as birds here are usually silent and invisible during windy weather. Sibbald Creek Trail is mostly gravel-surfaced, and can be rough in places. In winter, the parking lots are usually closed to vehicles by barricades or deep snow. Please note: neither gasoline nor food are available along Sibbald Creek Trail.

Heading west on the Trans-Canada Highway, 35 km from Canada Olympic Park, watch for the Sibbald Creek Trail exit (Hwy 68) marked by a large green-and–white sign. Decelerate fairly rapidly as there is a stop sign and Texas gate at the end of the ramp. Turn right and park close to the fencewire gate overlooking the small pond **(Trans-Canada/ Sibbald Creek Trail pond)** fringed with cattails and poplars. During spring migration from late March to mid-April, this pond is perhaps the most reliable place in the Calgary Region for Trumpeter Swan. Tundra Swans occasionally stop here too, making comparison possible at close range, especially if you have a scope. Barrow's Goldeneye is a common spring migrant and this is also the time to watch for both Bald and Golden Eagles nearby. Summer residents include Pied-billed Grebe, Canada Goose, Mallard, Canvasback, Ring-necked Duck (uncommon), Sora, American Coot, Black Tern, and Red-winged Blackbird. The air above the pond swarms with Cliff Swallows which

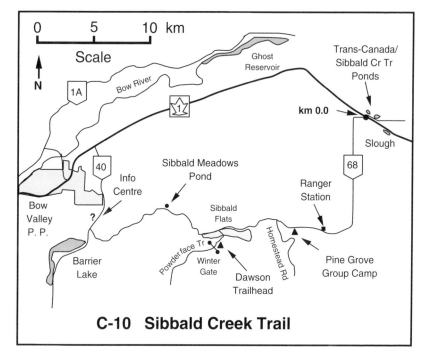

C-10 Sibbald Creek Trail

nest under the nearby highway overpass. You may also wish to check
the small slough 0.7 km to the east along the gravel road.

Distances are given from the Trans-Canada Highway to access points
and do not include side trips. From the overpass (**km 0.0**) head south
on Sibbald Creek Trail past the entrance to a natural gas processing
plant. In this area, there are post-mounted signs warning of potential
Hydrogen Sulphide (H_2S) emissions from nearby wells and pumping
stations. Although the hazard is small, do not enter private roadways
off Sibbald Creek Trail without permission.

After 3.5 km mixed woods cover a diagonal series of small ridges
which have in past years been home to Northern Pygmy-Owl, Barred
Owl and Great Gray Owl. For traffic safety reasons, stop to listen for
bird calls only in clearly visible areas, such as near the T-intersection
(4.1 km). You may hear only the chatter of Red Squirrels, but other
mammals such as Mule Deer, Moose, Coyote, Black Bear and Cougar
also wander throughout these ridges and the small marshes between
them.

In late May and early June of 1988, during a particularly dry spring elsewhere, several birders saw one Yellow Rail and heard others at a small grassy marsh (7.5 km)—the first time this species had been reported in the Calgary Region since the 1950s; Swamp Sparrow was present as well. These foothills marshes and their environs regularly attract such species as Red-tailed Hawk, Ruffed Grouse, Sora, Lesser Yellowlegs, Common Snipe, Yellow-bellied Sapsucker, Alder Flycatcher, Common Raven, Yellow Warbler, Common Yellowthroat, Le Conte's Sparrow, White-throated Sparrow, Red-winged Blackbird and Pine Siskin.

Another Texas gate (12 km) marks the eastern boundary of Kananaskis Country. Conifers dominate from the Ranger Station (12.5 km) westward to the mountains. Northern Goshawk; Northern Pygmy- (usually present at the top of the hill, just past the Ranger Station), Barred, Great Gray, Boreal and Northern Saw-whet Owls; and Pileated Woodpecker are scarce and elusive residents of this area. Varied Thrush occurs in summer. Steep-sided places along Jumping Pound and similar creeks should be checked for Western Flycatcher.

At the **Pine Grove Group Camp** (15.7 km) small meadows, willows and aspens attract Willow Flycatcher, migrant warblers and sparrows. The first 2 km south on Homestead Road (16.5 km; also marked by a sign for the provincial Rifle Association firing range) have been considered fairly reliable for the locally uncommon Boreal Owl and Red Crossbill, although logging activity further south in this mature coniferous forest may change this status. Continuing on Sibbald Creek Trail, Northern Saw-whet Owls are routinely heard from the Bateman Creek Texas gate (19.8 km) to the Powderface Trail. The Sibbald Viewpoint (20.8 km) offers a spectacular view of the foothills; Gray Jays may visit during a picnic here.

Powderface Trail (23.2 km), a logging road which runs for 34 km in a southerly direction between Sibbald Creek Trail and Elbow Falls Trail, first crosses a large marshy meadow area known as **Sibbald Flats**. In winter, this area can be good for Great Gray Owl and in late April the alpine race of the Horned Lark is plentiful here, waiting for the alpine meadows to thaw out. 3 km south of the Sibbald/Powderface intersection on Powderface Trail is the Dawson Equestrian Campground. The **Dawson Hiking Trail** has deciduous trees on south-facing slopes and conifers on the northern sides and ridgetops. Red-tailed Hawk,

Spruce Grouse, Northern Pygmy-Owl, both Yellow-bellied and Red-naped Sapsuckers, Olive-sided Flycatcher, Winter Wren, Swainson's Thrush, MacGillivray's Warbler, and Red Crossbill may be found in this general area. Note: Powderface Trail is closed beyond this point from December lst to May 15th each year.

Continuing along Sibbald Creek Trail the valley now narrows so that the road closely parallels Sibbald Creek, impeded at this point by a series of beaver dams. Typical birds in this quasi-canyon are Northern Goshawk, Common Raven, Boreal Chickadee, Common Yellowthroat, Wilson's Warbler and Fox Sparrow (uncommon). Owls are occasionally heard west of the Crane Meadows Picnic Area and Texas gate (27.7 km). In summer, the Sibbald Meadows Pond (29.7 km) is extremely popular with picnickers and fishermen, but has few birds.

The first view of a mountain also marks the beginning of the Kananaskis River watershed (32.1 km). The route now descends gradually to Hwy 40 (37.3 km). Along the way are Stony Creek and Lusk Creek parking areas and hiking trails. The thick tree cover here is almost completely coniferous. At the intersection with Hwy 40, a left turn will take you into the Kananaskis Valley (see routes C-11 and C-12), while a right turn (north) will take you to the Trans-Canada Highway in about 7 km. Mountain Chickadee can usually be found in the woods around this intersection in winter.

The Barrier Lake Information Centre, one kilometre north of the intersection, is open from 9:00 a.m. to 4:00 p.m. year-round except on Mondays and Tuesdays during winter. Maps and information on Kananaskis Country are available here, as well as heated washrooms and a pay telephone.

Owling success on this route is entirely weather-dependent during the peak season from mid-March to late April. It is essential to pick a *clear, near-calm* night since cloud cover inhibits the owls' inclination to call, and wind affects both human and owl ability to hear. It may not be essential to have a full moon to encourage the owls to call, but it certainly helps human visual orientation. The moonlit landscape takes on an eerie beauty, while the Milky Way and orbiting satellites can be seen clearly. Dress warmly since it is amazing how cold you can become after getting out of your vehicle a few times.

The area between the Ranger Station and Sibbald Meadows Pond typi-cally produces the largest number of calling owls. If the owls do not call spontaneously within a few minutes of stopping your vehicle and getting out, go on to the next stop. Cassette recordings seldom seem to stimulate owl vocalizations in our area. In the Calgary Region, North-ern Pygmy-Owls give single toots and do not respond to the double toots featured on most commercial tapes. The vocal range of the small owls on calm nights appears to be less than one kilometre. By mid-April, snow cover is melting rapidly and Common Snipe arrive at the small roadside sloughs. Their late-night courtship flights produce a sound, "winnowing", which can be vaguely similar to the rapid hoots of the Boreal Owl—inexperienced birders can be fooled by this.

On the return trip (eastbound) along the Trans-Canada Highway, 3 km east of the Sibbald Creek Trail intersection, watch for a small rocky ridge topped by a few short conifers on the left (north) side of the highway. Golden Eagles, buteos or ravens may be seen here, either perched on the rocks or hovering in the air flow deflected above the ridge. On the south side of the highway a long, narrow pond parallels the road. This is the first prairie-type slough east of the foothills along the Trans-Canada and features most of the common prairie ducks throughout the summer as well as a small nesting population of Black Terns. Pull well off the highway beyond the guardrails to scope the slough. Lesser Yellowlegs and Spotted Sandpiper are the shorebirds most likely to be seen, and four types of swallows (Barn, Tree, North-ern Rough-winged and Cliff) are regular visitors. Swainson's and Red-tailed Hawks are often seen nearby.

ROSS DICKSON

C-11 The Kananaskis Valley

Kananaskis Country is a vast, scenic recreation area on the eastern slope of the Rocky Mountains. This route samples some of the birding possibilities from its northern boundary near the Trans-Canada Highway, south through the Kananaskis River valley to Peter Lougheed Provincial Park. The vegetation consists mainly of young to

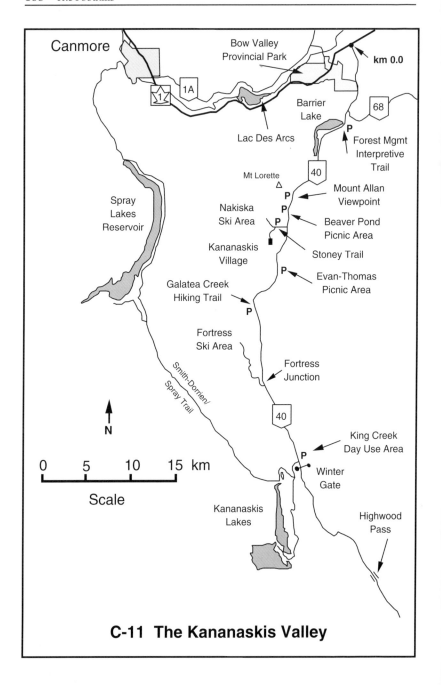

C-11 The Kananaskis Valley

intermediate growth Lodgepole Pine and spruce, with aspens and low willows near water. A few pockets of old growth forest remain, generally in wetter areas. There are several large lakes, extensive wetlands and numerous creeks. Along the highway elevations are around 1,675 m (5,500 ft); hiking trails can be followed higher into subalpine areas. Be prepared for unpredictable mountain weather. Even if you are starting out on a warm, sunny summer's day, rain and cold winds can begin with little warning. Some trails may not be clear of snow until early June. Most people, including birders, visit the Kananaskis to enjoy the magnificent scenery. Birds do not occur in any great density and finding montane specialties usually requires some physical effort. In winter, this is one of the few places in the Region where Steller's Jay might be found, especially around the parking areas in Peter Lougheed Provincial Park. Note: Hwy 40 is closed south of the park from December 1 to June 15 each year.

The route begins at the junction of the Trans-Canada Highway and Hwy 40 (Kananaskis Trail), 61.2 km west of Canada Olympic Park. As you begin driving south on Hwy 40, set your odometer at the Texas gate immediately south of the overpass (**km 0.0**). All distances are given from here to the access points and do not include side trips.

After 8.7 km the northern end of **Barrier Lake** will be seen to your right. This cold, deep reservoir is lacking in nutrients and does not attract many waterfowl. In late fall however, it should be checked for loons and Surf Scoter. Black Scoter has been recorded in the vicinity of the dam. Opposite Barrier Lake is the Kananaskis Centre for Environmental Research (9.1 km). Here, the 2.3 km **Forest Management Interpretive Trail** can be worth walking. Spruce Grouse is an elusive resident of the area and it can also be good for Red Crossbill when there is an abundant cone crop. Enquire at the buildings for the location of any feeders, especially in early summer for hummingbirds.

During the last half of March and early April, Golden Eagles migrate in a northwesterly direction across the Kananaskis Valley from the Fisher Range to Mt Lorette. Counts of more than 200 eagles a day have been recorded. The **Mt Allan Viewpoint** (20 km) is a good location for viewing this migration. The birds will be at mountain top height, so a telescope will be an asset. Fall migration peaks in late September and early October. Up to 500 raptors a day have been observed at this time, mainly Golden Eagles but also including Bald

Eagle, Sharp-shinned Hawk and Northern Goshawk. On May 24, 1992 two Vaux's Swifts were observed near Mt Allan.

A stroll along the footpaths at the **Beaver Pond Picnic Area** (21 km) can be rewarding, especially in the early morning or evening. Watch for the trail sign to the bridge, half way along the parking lot. Species of note to listen for include Varied Thrush and Townsend's Warbler.

The Nakiska Ski Area road (23 km) provides access to a good birding area in the vicinity of Mt Lorette. Follow the Nakiska road across the Kananaskis River, continue for a further kilometre and park in the **Stoney Trail** parking area. It can be worthwhile following this equestrian trail for 3 or 4 kilometres to Mt Lorette Creek. Species to watch and listen for in appropriate habitat include: Harlequin Duck; Alder, Willow, Least, Dusky (the most widespread empid. in this area) and Western Flycatchers; Winter Wren; Fox Sparrow; and Cassin's Finch (rare). Black Swifts were regular in the area throughout the summer of 1992, with flocks of up to 8 birds being present. Check for migrant Swamp Sparrows in October; American Dipper can be abundant in winter.

Northern Pygmy-Owl and Boreal Owl have been heard calling at night from April to July at **Evan-Thomas Creek** (27.3 km).

From the **Galatea Creek** parking lot (32.6 km) an excellent hiking trail parallels the creek and it is worthwhile following this for a few kilometres. Breeding species to watch for in this area include Golden Eagle, Rufous Hummingbird, Western Flycatcher, Hermit Thrush, Varied Thrush and Townsend's Warbler.

At Fortress Junction (41.5 km), a drive up to the **Fortress Mountain Ski Area** offers easy access to subalpine habitat. There are no formal trails, but some time spent hiking at tree line should produce Brewer's, Fox and White-crowned Sparrows.

Just before the winter barrier watch for the **King Creek Day Use Area** on the left-hand side of the highway (49.9 km). Here, a short (about 1 km) hiking trail can be followed up the steep-walled canyon. This is one of the few reliable locations in the Region for Winter Wren. Listen for its loud, bubbly song coming from near the ground in dense undergrowth. American Dipper can be found here too, and Steller's Jay has been seen higher up the canyon in fall.

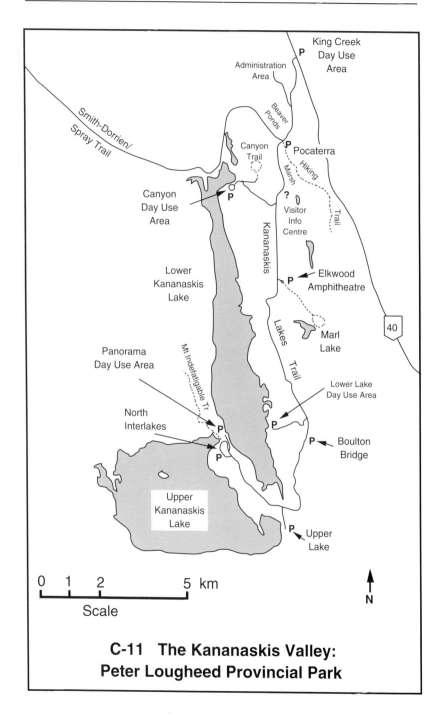

0 1 2   5 km
Scale

N

C-11 The Kananaskis Valley:
Peter Lougheed Provincial Park

Turn right at 50 km onto **Kananaskis Lakes Trail.** The service road on the right (51.2 km) leads to the Administration area. Just south of the Administration building is a large shrub meadow. Calliope Hummingbird can occasionally be found here in the willows. This area is also good for Ruffed Grouse, Varied Thrush, warblers and sparrows. Boreal Owl has been heard calling in this general area in spring.

Pocaterra can be a productive area. Park in the Pocaterra parking lot on the left-hand side of the road (52.2 km). The **Pocaterra Trail** begins just southeast of Pocaterra Hut. A hike of two to three kilometres would expose you to most of the habitat possibilities. Open brushy areas along the creek produce the most sightings. Watch for Harlequin Duck whenever you have a good view of the water. Both Calliope and Rufous Hummingbirds are possibilities—keep your eyes and ears open at extensive areas of flowers, particularly Indian Paint Brush. Don't forget to look up occasionally as this is another location in the Kananaskis where Black Swift has been sighted, particularly towards evening. Other species to watch for include: Spruce Grouse, Spotted Sandpiper, Common Snipe, Belted Kingfisher, Gray Jay, Boreal Chickadee, both kinglets, Swainson's Thrush, Varied Thrush, MacGillivray's Warbler, Wilson's Warbler and Lincoln's Sparrow. Many ski trails criss-cross the area and if you intend to leave the main trail you should carry the winter ski trail map.

Pocaterra "Beaver Ponds" There is an extensive swampy area with numerous beaver ponds and pockets of old growth forest on the west side of Kananaskis Lakes Trail. From the Pocaterra parking lot walk a short distance back up the road to the bridge over Pocaterra Creek and follow it westwards. Shortly after passing the power line clearing you come to an old exploration road running northward from the creek. Use the road only if it is not too wet. Many of the species mentioned for Pocaterra Trail occur here too. Watch also for Barrow's Goldeneye, Ruffed Grouse and Northern Waterthrush.

Pocaterra "Marsh" This is the northern end of a long, narrow marshy trench which extends southwards from the parking area for almost 4 km. Good observations can be made from the road and it is worthwhile walking south to the top of the ridge. Leave your vehicle in the parking lot as there is no safe place to park along the roadside. A scope will be an asset. Watch for Ring-necked Duck, Barrow's Goldeneye, Bufflehead and Hooded Merganser (uncommon). In spring, check the shrubby area across the road for kinglets and warblers.

Park maps and information can be obtained at the Visitor Information
Centre (53.6 km). Birders should be aware that, while remote, the
possibility of encountering a bear does exist. If you are a newcomer to
"Bear Country" an informative brochure can be obtained here. The
staff will also have information on any temporary trail closures due to
bear activity.

The access road to the Canyon area is on the right, about 400 m
beyond the Visitor Information Centre. The access road divides after
about a kilometre. If you take the left fork you will come to the
Canyon Day Use Area where a good view of the northern end of
Lower Kananaskis Lake can be obtained. More of the lake can be
viewed by walking south from the parking area on Lower Lake Trail.
Both Upper and Lower Kananaskis Lakes were once true lakes but in
the 1950s hydro plants were constructed at their outflow points and
water levels became artificially controlled. In spring, water levels are
very low and the lakes resemble large, partially flooded gravel pits.
They are allowed to fill up somewhat over the summer. Consequently,
fewer waterbirds will be seen in spring, but from late summer
onwards the lakes host respectable numbers of loons, grebes, ducks
and gulls.

If you bear right at the access road fork you will come to the Canyon
camping area. This can be worth checking during migration for small
passerines. The **Kananaskis Canyon Interpretive Trail** (0.8 km long)
follows the wooded ridge and then heads down into the canyon itself.
As the lake outflow has been diverted into a penstock the "river" is
now little more than a creek, dry in places. There is enough water to
attract nesting American Dippers however, and Western Flycatcher
can usually be found here too.

The **Marl Lake Interpretive Trail** is accessed by parking at the Elkwood Amphitheatre (55.9 km). The first part of this 2.5 km trail trav-
erses the Elkwood Campground and can be hard to follow. On the
way to Marl Lake watch for Sharp-shinned Hawk, Spruce Grouse and
Varied Thrush. At the lake you may see Ring-necked Duck, Barrow's
Goldeneye and (occasionally) Bald Eagle.

A marshy pond area borders Kananaskis Lakes Trail at 56.6 km. The
safest way to check out this area is to park on the Service Road. The
main pond can be reached by walking north for a few metres and

taking the gravel trail towards William Watson Lodge. After about 100 m cut south for 50 m to the pond. The usual waterfowl and marsh species can be expected. Greater Scaup has been seen here in May.

Boulton Creek can be good for both breeding species and fall migrants. A good place to park for birding the estuary and shoreline is the Lower Lake Day Use Area (59.8 km). Birding is good along the creek from the highway to the lake and it is worthwhile walking the system of paths throughout the area. The willows around the mouth of Boulton Creek have been good for Willow Flycatcher. Orange-crowned, Yellow-rumped, and Wilson's Warblers nest in the area and by mid-August mixed flocks of warblers begin moving south through the shrubbery along the shoreline. This is also a good area for waterbirds in fall. The creek is good east of the highway too. Park at **Boulton Bridge** (60.2 km) and follow the Boulton Creek Interpretive Trail which begins here. The loop is 5 km in length but you may prefer just to walk the sections on either side of the creek. Watch for Spruce Grouse, flycatchers, American Dipper, thrushes and warblers.

From late summer onwards it can be worthwhile stopping at **Upper Lake** (62.6 km) to check out the waterbirds on Upper Kananaskis Lake.

After crossing the isthmus between the two lakes you come to the **Panorama Day Use Area** (65.3 km). You will now have a good view of the southern end of Lower Kananaskis Lake. Lighting is best here later in the day. Common Loon and Harlequin Duck have been seen here in May but again, waterbird numbers will be greater in fall.

As you leave the Panorama access road, turning right will bring you to the end of Kananaskis Lakes Trail at the **North Interlakes** parking area (65.9 km). This will give you another view of Upper Kananaskis Lake. Several hiking trails begin here and if you are feeling ambitious and have the time, taking a hike up the **Mt Indefatigable Trail** is well worth the effort, both from the variety of habitat this will expose you to as well as the spectacular view of the whole valley. It is 3.8 km to the first viewpoint, but it is very steep in places, with the end being at about 2,135 m (7,000 ft). Blue Grouse can be heard booming in May along the ridge on the west side of the trail. Rufous Hummingbird and Townsend's Solitaire may also be seen from this trail.

Gas can be obtained at the Fortress Junction Service Centre. Snacks
are available at Fortress Junction and Boulton Trading Post and restau-
rant meals at the hotels in Kananaskis Village. Full tourist facilities are
available in Canmore.

GARY CLARKE

C-12 The Highwood Valley

The drive from Longview to the Highwood Pass is one of the most
beautiful in southern Alberta, starting on the prairies and ending at
the highest pass in Canada that can be driven. The road is an excellent paved highway with picnic areas, campgrounds and hiking
trails giving the birder access to a wide variety of foothill, subalpine
and alpine habitats. White-tailed Ptarmigan, Calliope Hummingbird and Lazuli Bunting are some of the sought-after species to be
looked for here. It should be noted that Hwy 40 (Kananaskis Trail)
is closed between Highwood Junction and Peter Lougheed Provincial Park (north of the Highwood Pass) from December 1 to June 15
each year.

To reach the start of this route, head south from Calgary on Hwy 2 and
take the Hwy 2A exit for Okotoks (see Section C map). Continue on
Hwy 2A for 11.5 km to the junction with Hwy 7. Turn right (west) on
Hwy 7 and drive for 19.3 km to Black Diamond, then turn left (south)
on Hwy 22 for 17.2 km to the junction with S.R. 541 (Highwood Trail)
in Longview.

Turn right (west) on S.R. 541 (**km 0.0**). All distances are given from
here to the access points and do not include side trips. Between 6.5
and 9 km a low ridge parallels the highway to the north. This is an
excellent location for migrant raptors, particularly from late March to
early May. Swainson's, Red-tailed and Rough-legged Hawks, Prairie
Falcon, and both Bald and Golden Eagles can all be expected. In some
years Golden Eagles summer in the area and it is worthwhile stopping
to check the ridge as they may often be seen resting on the ground.

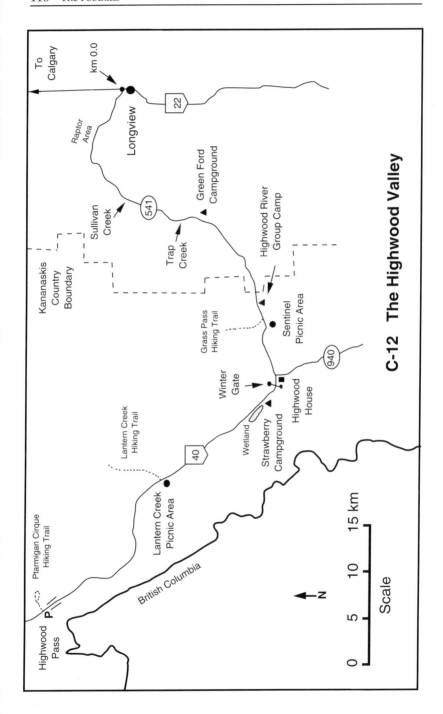

C-12 The Highwood Valley

In this section the valley and rolling hills are a mosaic of open pastures and aspen woodland. Mountain Bluebird is an early migrant and may be seen along the highway by the end of March. Lewis' Woodpecker has been observed in this part of the valley. Good stopping points along the highway are at Sullivan Creek (14.8 km), Trap Creek (21.4 km), and at Green Ford Campground (24 km). Species to watch for at these locations include: Western Wood-Pewee; Alder, Least and Western Flycatchers; Eastern Phoebe; Eastern Kingbird; American Dipper; Warbling Vireo; Tennessee and Yellow Warblers; Chipping, Clay-colored, Vesper, Savannah, Song, Lincoln's and White-crowned Sparrows; Red-winged and Brewer's Blackbirds; Northern Oriole; Pine Siskin; and American Goldfinch. Check all sapsuckers carefully– they may be either Yellow-bellied or Red-naped.

At 34 km the "Kananaskis Country" sign marks the boundary of the Forest Reserve; this is public land with free access. The area is home to Mule Deer, Elk, Bighorn Sheep, Cougar, Coyote and both Black and Grizzly Bears. Birders hiking in this area should be aware that the hunting season for large game extends from the beginning of April to mid-May and from the last week of August to the end of November; shooting is not permitted within 365 metres of the highway.

The stretch between the Kananaskis Country boundary and Highwood Junction runs between grassy hillsides dotted with clumps of aspen on the north side of the road and scrubland with Balsam Poplars and some spruce stands along the valley floor to the south. MacGillivray's Warbler and Lazuli Bunting frequent the aspen clumps, while Rufous Hummingbird, Dusky Flycatcher, Warbling Vireo and White-crowned Sparrow can be found in the poplars and scrub. The spruce stands may contain Sharp-shinned Hawk, Yellow-rumped Warbler, Northern Waterthrush and Wilson's Warbler. Harlequin Duck, Common Merganser, Spotted Sandpiper and American Dipper may be seen along the river. Several picnic areas with parking places and toilets are located along this stretch, providing convenient access points. The **Highwood River Group Camp and Picnic Area** immediately after the Kananaskis Country sign is a good location for Lazuli Bunting, the best time for finding this species being late June.

At 37.8 km, on the north side of the road 200 m before the Sentinel Picnic Area, is the hiking trail to **Grass Pass** and the Bull Creek Hills. There is no trail marker, so watch for a rocky track heading upslope.

This is easy year-round hiking in open country that is home to Northern Goshawk, Clark's Nutcracker, Common Raven, Mountain Chickadee, Townsend's Solitaire and American Pipit. In winter, White-tailed Ptarmigan and Snow Bunting have been found along the ridge tops at Grass Pass.

At **Highwood Junction** (43.5 km) the road becomes the Kananaskis Trail (Hwy 40). The convenience store at Highwood House usually has an active hummingbird feeder which may be visited by both Calliope and Rufous Hummingbirds. A large colony of Cliff Swallows nests beneath the road bridge just south of the junction and Willow Flycatcher can occur along the riverbank. Listen too for Pileated Woodpecker.

There is an extensive wetland complex, formed by the action of beavers, on the left as the road climbs the hill (48 km) just after **Strawberry Campground.** This is good for Common Snipe; Calliope Hummingbird; Willow Flycatcher; Yellow Warbler; Northern Waterthrush; MacGillivray's Warbler; Common Yellowthroat; Wilson's Warbler; and Song, Lincoln's and White-crowned Sparrows.

The highway continues north, still in the Highwood valley, with the magnificent peaks of the Continental Divide to the west and the High-wood Range to the east. There are several day-use areas and camp-grounds and from these are trails to the river and longer ones into the mountains for the more energetic. The **Lantern Creek Trail** (60.8 km), a strenuous 5 km hike to the tree line at Picklejar Lakes, can be reward-ing in late June. In addition to the common mountain warblers and sparrows, watch for Northern Goshawk, Golden Eagle, Spruce Grouse, Ruffed Grouse, Olive-sided Flycatcher, Western Flycatcher, Steller's Jay, Clark's Nutcracker, Hermit Thrush, and both crossbills.

After about 70 km the road starts to climb to the **Highwood Pass**, which is reached at 81.5 km. Varied Thrush and Chipping, Fox and White-crowned Sparrows can sometimes be seen along the interpre-tive trail at the parking area. Follow this trail across the road to **Ptarmigan Cirque**, a 2.5 km hike climbing 230 metres into the alpine zone. The height is gained in the first kilometre, the trail then emerg-ing from the trees into an alpine valley with superb views and which in July and August is filled with flowers. Species to watch for on this hike include White-tailed Ptarmigan (elusive; most easily located in fall after the first snows when their tracks may be followed), Clark's Nutcracker, Mountain Chickadee, American Pipit and Rosy Finch.

From Highwood Pass you can either retrace the route or continue on Hwy 40 (see route C-11) for some 65 km to the Trans-Canada Highway for the return to Calgary.

Gas and meals can be obtained in Longview. Highwood House has a Park Ranger Office and Information Centre (558–2151), a seasonal gas station and a convenience store serving quality snack foods; these are closed in winter.

RICHARD CLARKE

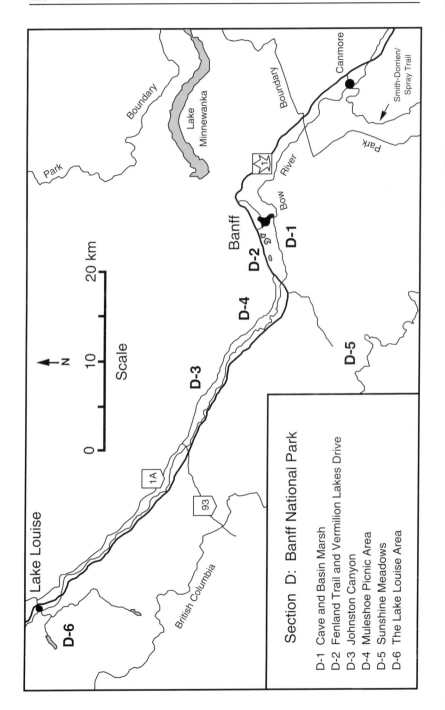

Section D: Banff National Park

D-1 Cave and Basin Marsh
D-2 Fenland Trail and Vermilion Lakes Drive
D-3 Johnston Canyon
D-4 Muleshoe Picnic Area
D-5 Sunshine Meadows
D-6 The Lake Louise Area

D-1 Cave and Basin Marsh

Any first-time birding trip to Banff National Park should begin with a visit to the main Information Centre (224 Banff Avenue, Banff; open: 8:00 a.m. to 10:00 p.m. daily, mid-June to Sept; 10:00 a.m. to 6:00 p.m. daily, rest of year) to pick up a bird checklist and the brochure entitled "Banff and Vicinity Drives and Walks" (includes Lake Louise), and to enquire about trail conditions and potential wildlife hazards. In Calgary call 292–4411 (weekdays, 8:00 a.m. to 4:30 p.m.) for park information. Getting around in and near Banff Townsite is easier on foot than by car.

To reach the Information Centre, westbound travellers on the Trans-Canada Highway (Hwy 1) should take the first Banff exit (approx. 12.5 km west of the park gate). Turn left at the stop sign, pass beneath Hwy 1 to a map of Banff Townsite (0.6 km) and continue southwest along this road—which becomes Banff Avenue. At the second traffic light (4.4 km), the Wolf Avenue junction, turn left and then take the first right (behind the church) to the parking lot for the Information Centre (4.5 km). If eastbound on the Trans-Canada, watch for the overpass above the east end of Hwy 1A (Bow Valley Parkway). At 4.2 km is the Vermilion Lakes overlook. Take the Banff/Mt Norquay exit (5.5 km), turn right and follow Mt Norquay Road into Banff. At 7 km turn left onto Wolf Avenue. Proceed to the Wolf/Banff Avenue stop light (7.2 km), carry straight on and (as above) take the first right (7.3 km) for the Information Centre parking lot. If you should miss your first Banff exit from the Trans-Canada, it is only 3.6 km to the second.

Directions to the **Cave and Basin Marsh** are given from downtown Banff. From the Banff Avenue/Wolf intersection head south on Banff Avenue across the Bow River bridge to the T-intersection in front of the Park Administration Building. The grounds of the Administration Building (the Cascade Gardens) are worth birding at any time of year. Turn right at the T-intersection onto Cave Avenue and continue to the Cave and Basin parking lot. Pedestrians can take the trail which starts on the right some 300 m along Cave Avenue, beyond the Luxton Museum. At the far (southwest) end of the parking lot look for a small hiking trail sign. Follow this trail (which joins the above-mentioned pathway) for about 75 m and then turn right onto the 0.5 km-long Marsh Trail boardwalk system. For wheelchair access, and to visit the

Cave and Basin Hot Springs Centennial Centre (where exhibits com-
memorate the birthplace of Banff National Park) and swimming pool,
take the paved pathway which starts just to the left of the hiking trail
sign. This site plus Fenland Trail and Vermilion Lakes Drive (D-2) can
be covered in half a day.

In good cone-crop years, noisy flocks of crossbills may decorate the
spruces around the parking lot. Key habitat elements at Cave and
Basin are the mixed spruce-pine forest, and a medium-sized lake with
its expanse of reed beds, waterside willow thickets and marshy borders. En route to the marsh check the spruce-pine forest for year-
round inhabitants such as Black-capped and Boreal Chickadees,
Brown Creeper and Golden-crowned Kinglet. Noteworthy summer
residents include Ruby-crowned Kinglet; a variety of warblers:
Orange-crowned, Townsend's, and Wilson's; White-crowned Sparrow;
and Dark-eyed Junco. Dawn is usually the most rewarding time of
day to bird here in the summer.

The lake and marsh can be scanned (take your scope) from several
points along the boardwalk, at the end of which are fish and bird-
viewing platforms. (At present, these platforms are not wheelchair
accessible.) Three introduced tropical fish species can be observed
but the Banff Long-nosed Dace, known only from this lake, may now
be extinct. Garter snakes also occur hereabouts. Summer residents
to watch for around the marsh and its environs include Belted Kingfisher; Olive-sided, Alder and Willow Flycatchers; American Redstart;
Common Yellowthroat; Savannah and Song Sparrows; and Red-
winged Blackbird. American Bittern also occurs but seeing one
requires patience and luck. Watch for six swallow species hawking
insects over the lake. Most waterfowl species common in the park,
including all three teal, have been seen here. In fall, the lake is regularly frequented by Hooded Merganser; Rusty Blackbird can be found
along the water's edge.

As a result of the hot springs' outflow, small portions of the lake (especially around the fish viewing platform) remain ice-free through the
winter. It is an excellent spot to check for a variety of overwintering
species such as Green-winged Teal, Mallard, American Wigeon,
Killdeer, Common Snipe, American Dipper, Song Sparrow and Rusty
Blackbird. Dress very warmly. Caution: During winter, the boardwalk and steps to the platforms can be extremely slippery.

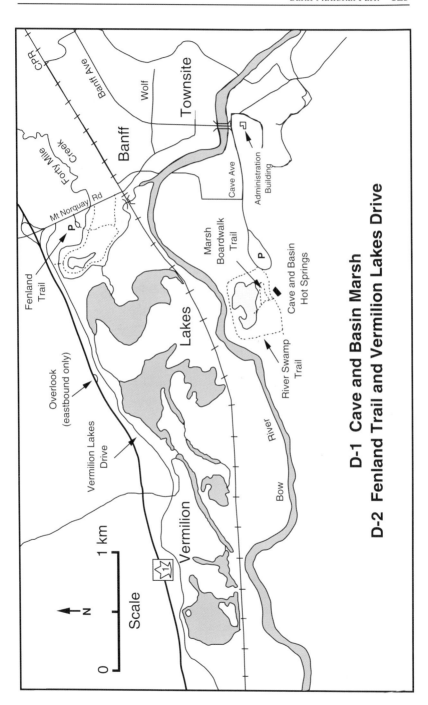

D-1 Cave and Basin Marsh
D-2 Fenland Trail and Vermilion Lakes Drive

The **River Swamp Trail**, a 2 km loop around the Cave and Basin Marsh, begins about halfway along the parking lot. If you have the time, it is well worth walking part or all of this. It is much quieter than the boardwalk but watch out for horse traffic and muddy patches. The trail passes through good wetland habitat and allows views of the Bow River. Have your insect repellent handy.

Food can be obtained at the Cave and Basin Centennial Centre coffee shop during the summer. Heated washrooms are available in the centre year-round.

RICHARD THOMAS and ROSS DICKSON

D-2 Fenland Trail and Vermilion Lakes Drive

Fenland Trail Located within the otherwise heavily-forested Bow River valley, the Fenland forms the eastern end of the Vermilion Lakes wetlands complex. A flat, wheelchair-accessible, 1.5 km loop trail along the banks of Forty Mile Creek allows visitors to observe a variety of woodland and wetland habitats. Sedges, rushes and grasses attract Elk and Moose to a series of shallow ponds which, together with the creeks and lakes of this area support populations of Beaver and Muskrat. The greatest abundance and diversity of birds occurs during the peak migration periods (mid- to late May, mid- to late August) and during June when the breeding species are singing. For best results, and to avoid most of the joggers and cyclists who frequent this popular trail, an early morning start is recommended.

To access Fenland Trail from the Trans-Canada Highway, take the Banff/Mt Norquay exit and start driving towards Banff Townsite. Almost immediately, on the right, is the start of Vermilion Lakes Drive. For now pass this and watch for the entrance to the Fenland parking lot, also on the right. For access from downtown Banff, start at the Wolf/Banff Avenue stop light. Go west on Wolf for 0.2 km to a stop sign. Turn right and follow this main road (signed "To the Trans-Canada Highway"); this becomes Mt Norquay Road. After crossing the railway tracks and Forty Mile Creek, watch for the Fenland sign and turn left into the parking lot. Pedestrians can enter the trail system on the west side of Mt Norquay Road, just beyond the railway tracks. At the main trailhead pick up the well-illustrated "Fenland Self-Guiding Trail" brochure.

Spruce stands are home year-round to Three-toed Woodpecker, Gray Jay, Boreal Chickadee, Red-breasted Nuthatch, Brown Creeper and Golden-crowned Kinglet. Evidence for the bark-flaking activities of Three-toed Woodpeckers (red patches on spruce trunks) is common but the birds themselves can be elusive. Pileated Woodpecker has been seen in the aspens and dead conifers between Forty Mile Creek and first Vermilion Lake. Look for American Dippers floating "phalarope-like" down the creek. On late winter/early spring evenings, listen for Northern Pygmy-, Barred and Boreal Owls. During spring and summer, migrant and breeding species to watch and listen for include: Alder and Willow Flycatchers; both kinglets; Swainson's and Varied Thrushes; Orange-crowned, Yellow-rumped, Townsend's and Wilson's Warblers; American Redstart; Common Yellowthroat; and Song, Lincoln's and White-crowned Sparrows. During winter, with luck, one may encounter Pine Grosbeak, White-winged Crossbill, Common Redpoll, Pine Siskin (rare) and Evening Grosbeak.

Caution: The fen is a calving area for Elk in late May and early June. The Elk may be in the vicinity of the trail, and may be dangerous. Do not approach these animals at this time or come between mother Elk and their young.

Vermilion Lakes Drive At the Fenland parking lot exit, turn left (north) onto Mt Norquay Road and drive about 0.2 km to the turnoff for Vermilion Lakes Drive (**km 0.0**). After 4.3 km this winding road dead-ends at a turnaround area. Points of note along the route are: at 0.5 km, a footbridge connecting the Drive to the Fenland Trail; 0.8 and 1.8 km, small pullouts for the first and second Vermilion Lakes, respectively; and 3.9 km, the sign for the third Vermilion Lake. Be cautious when driving this route as it is narrow in places and extremely popular with joggers and cyclists.

The Bow Valley is a significant migration corridor and the three shallow Vermilion Lakes, together with their interconnecting network of channels and marshes, constitute one of the most important stopover points for migrant waterfowl within Banff National Park. Of ecological importance, in addition to the lakes and marshes, are stands of mature spruce, birch and young aspens and extensive willow thickets. For migrant and breeding passerines the areas from the Drive entrance to the first lake, and between the second and third lakes are best. Large mammals seen regularly in the Vermilion Lakes vicinity include Elk, Moose and Bighorn Sheep.

Peak periods for migrant waterfowl are late April and May, and mid-August to late September. All of Banff's regularly-occurring grebes, herons and ducks have been seen in this general area. Interesting duck species to watch for include Cinnamon Teal, Surf Scoter, Barrow's Goldeneye and Hooded Merganser. Any Tundra or Trumpeter Swans will be migrants but Red-necked Grebe has bred at the third lake. First Vermilion Lake usually hosts a pair of Ospreys and a pair of Bald Eagles—both locally rare as breeding species. Look for their massive nests in the tall, dead conifers. Cooper's Hawk has nested at third Vermilion Lake. In summer, dawn-chorus contributors from lakeside thickets may include: Alder Flycatcher, Warbling Vireo, Red-eyed Vireo, Yellow Warbler, Northern Waterthrush, MacGillivray's Warbler, Common Yellowthroat, Wilson's Warbler, and Song and Lincoln's Sparrows. During August, these species together with Tennessee and Orange-crowned Warblers and a variety of sparrows sometimes "fill" the aspen and willow scrub along the Drive. The birds may stop near the network of beaver dams and canals for a drink and a bath. Fall migration often brings Common Terns to feed and rest at the second lake. In winter, Snow Bunting and Common Redpoll have been recorded along the Drive and American Dippers are sometimes found at warm spring-related, ice-free patches of the third lake. Listen overhead for Clark's Nutcracker and Common Raven year-round.

It is also worthwhile stopping at the **Vermilion Lakes Overlook**, accessible only from the eastbound lane of the Trans-Canada Highway. If westbound on the Trans-Canada, use the Hwy 1A (Bow Valley Parkway) exit, 5.5 km west of the Banff Townsite/Mt Norquay interchange, to reverse course. In addition to a panorama of the lakes (use your scope here), this overlook affords a superb view of highly photogenic Mt Rundle.

RICHARD THOMAS

D-3 Johnston Canyon

Johnston Canyon is a narrow, steep-sided gorge located adjacent to Hwy 1A (the Bow Valley Parkway), just east of Eisenhower Junction. It is one of the most popular (and most crowded) short hikes in Banff National Park. The magnet which draws birders however, is not the pleasant scenery but a small breeding colony of Black Swifts. Winter Wren can also be found here, plus several montane species which are sometimes difficult to find elsewhere. The swifts arrive at the beginning of June and may be observed until early September, when the young fledge. Early morning is the best time to bird the canyon as the crowds start to build up by ten. To see the swifts flying, time your visit to just before dusk. With an early start, Johnston Canyon can be combined with a visit to the Lake Louise area (D-6).

To reach Johnston Canyon drive west for about 5.5 km on the Trans-Canada Highway (Hwy 1) from the Banff Townsite/Mt Norquay interchange, and exit to the right onto Hwy 1A (the Bow Valley Parkway). Continue for 17.8 km and park in the public parking lot on the right, just east of the Johnston Canyon Resort complex. Eastbound travellers on the Trans-Canada can take the Hwy 93 exit. In this case, go north for 1.5 km and turn right onto Hwy 1A and drive a further 6.4 km to the parking lot. Along the Bow Valley Parkway watch for both Three-toed and Pileated Woodpeckers. Occasionally, Blue Grouse may be seen beside the highway in early spring. At the lodge, check the ornamental flowers and the occasional feeder for Rufous Hummingbird.

The trail to the Lower Falls has a mild uphill grade; the distance is approximately 1.6 km return. To the Upper Falls it is 4.8 km return. The trail winds through a moist, mature forest of Lodgepole Pine and Engelmann Spruce beside noisy Johnston Creek. Hearing birds can sometimes be a challenge. At the narrowest point the path is carried by means of a suspended walkway bolted to the canyon wall. American Dipper should be seen along the creek—in recent years it has nested near the Lower Falls. About half-way to the Lower Falls, on the opposite side of the creek, watch for a rock fall with the scattered remains of many fallen trees. This is one of the best locations for finding Winter Wren.

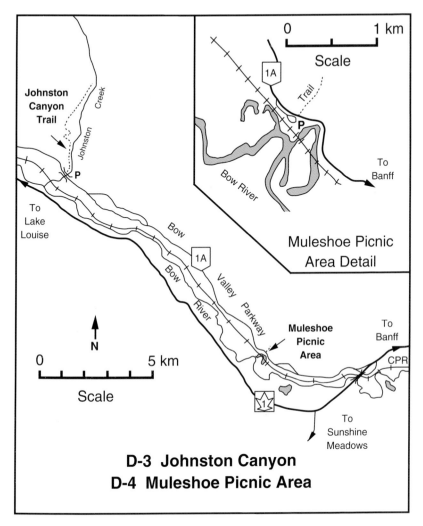

Johnston Canyon Trail

To Lake Louise

To Banff

Muleshoe Picnic Area Detail

0   1 km
Scale

Bow River

Trail

N

0   5 km
Scale

Bow Valley Parkway

Bow River

Muleshoe Picnic Area

To Banff

CPR

To Sunshine Meadows

D-3 Johnston Canyon
D-4 Muleshoe Picnic Area

Check for Western Flycatcher as you approach the suspended walk-way; Townsend's Solitaire usually nests on the cliff face in this area too. Several Black Swift nests are located in the vicinity of the Lower Falls. They are always in inaccessible, and often wet places (look for patches of green slime), on the canyon walls but good views can be obtained from the trail. From the bridge at the falls, facing upstream, scan the rock face to the left of the falls. This is usually the most visi-ble nest. Others might be observed from the trail above the falls. Only one egg is laid and the young hatch towards the end of July. Swifts are rarely seen flying in the canyon during daylight hours as food is usually brought at dusk.

Above the falls, bird species typical of mature coniferous forest can be heard along the trail. Watch for the difficult to see Townsend's Warbler, the common Yellow-rumped Warbler and species such as crossbills. Further up the trail you may find Spruce Grouse.

Washrooms are located at the parking lot. Gas and food can be obtained at Johnston Canyon Resort.

DAVE ELPHINSTONE

D-4 Muleshoe Picnic Area

To reach this location, drive west on the Trans-Canada Highway (Hwy 1) for about 5.5 km from the Banff Townsite/Mt Norquay interchange and exit to the right onto Hwy 1A (the Bow Valley Parkway). Follow this road west for a further 5.5 km to a large parking area on the left side of the road, well-marked "Muleshoe Picnic Area". There are washrooms and several picnic tables on a small hill overlooking Muleshoe Lake, an oxbow cut-off of the Bow River. The vegetation between the road and the lake and river consists of a mixture of poplar, spruce and shrubbery. On the other (north) side of the road the slopes of Mt Cory ascend steeply, the aspens soon thin out and large patches of open alpine meadow appear between the stands of conifer.

The main birding interest at the Muleshoe Picnic Area is the reliability of finding Hammond's Flycatcher. This species occurs in aspens on the steep slopes above the road and on the edges of the alpine meadows. It is often not necessary to climb very far, since they may occur within a couple of hundred metres of the road. However, if you cannot find one that low down walk up the slope until the song is heard. June and the first few days of July is the season when they sing most consistently, but they are present until mid-August and usually perch in fairly prominent places. The only other Empidonax that is known to occur in the vicinity is Willow Flycatcher which might be found near the lake, but which has a completely different song.

Another bird of the mountain slopes is the Blue Grouse which may be heard hooting from mid-April to mid-June. The sound is actually a low, echoing series of "AROOMPH AROOMPH AROOMPH" sounds, a bit like a distant foghorn blowing short blasts. There is a definite ventriloquial quality to the call and it may be quite difficult to track down the displaying male bird. With persistence he should be found eventually, hooting from a conifer, a log or even from the ground.

Other birds that may be found on the steep slopes are: Spruce Grouse (very tame but hard to find), Pileated Woodpecker, Gray Jay, Clark's Nutcracker, Common Raven, Mountain Chickadee, Boreal Chickadee, Red-Breasted Nuthatch, Brown Creeper, Winter Wren, both kinglets, Townsend's Solitaire, Hermit Thrush, Varied Thrush, Townsend's Warbler, Fox Sparrow (near timberline), and White-winged Crossbill. Around Muleshoe Lake a broader range of birds is to be expected, including Violet-green Swallow, American Redstart, Northern Waterthrush, Common Yellowthroat and Wilson's Warbler.

Muleshoe Picnic Area is situated midway between Fenland Trail (D-2) and Johnston Canyon (D-3) and may be visited in combination with either or both of these locations.

ANDREW SLATER

D-5 Sunshine Meadows

Sunshine Meadows, one of the most easily accessible large areas of alpine meadow habitat in the Region, are located astride the Continental Divide between Alberta and British Columbia, about 18 km directly southwest of the Banff Townsite. Access to this alpine habitat is by an enclosed gondola, usually operational from 9:30 a.m. to 8:00 p.m. from June 30th through the Labour Day weekend in September (check with the Banff Information Centre 762–4256). It reopens from November to May for the ski season. The best times for birding at Sunshine are in early July when territorial

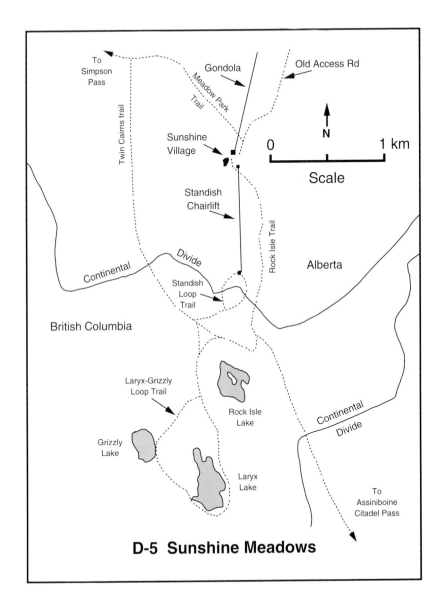

D-5 Sunshine Meadows

males are singing and from mid-August to early September during migration. Apart from the magnificent scenery, the main attraction for birders is the chance of finding White-tailed Ptarmigan and Rosy Finch. Allow a full day to do justice to this interesting area.

From the Mt Norquay/Banff Townsite interchange on the Trans-Canada Highway (Hwy 1) drive west for 7.3 km and exit to the right onto the well-signposted Sunshine access road. Follow this road for a further 9.6 km to the parking lot. As you drive watch for the occasional Spruce Grouse crossing the road, as well as Bighorn Sheep, Elk, and on rare occasions, Black Bear.

Although one can hike the 7 km up the old access road to Sunshine Village at the edge of the meadows, it is recommended that you take the 20 minute gondola ride. En route listen for Swainson's, Hermit and Varied Thrushes. Once at the village proceed to the Visitor Centre (the log building near the ski lifts) to obtain information and area trail maps. Although the staff's knowledge of birds is limited, they keep a list of recent sightings that could help locate specific species. Gray Jay, Clark's Nutcracker and Common Raven may be seen in the village area at any time. Look for Barn Swallow nests in the Day Lodge porch. From the village a system of well-graded, hardened trails takes the birder out into the subalpine and alpine habitats that surround the village. Visitors to the meadows are requested to stay on these trails to protect the fragile alpine vegetation.

The main trail (**Rock Isle Lake/Twin Cairns/Meadow Park Loop**) starts just south of the Visitor Centre. It runs in a clockwise direction past Rock Isle Lake, continues west of the ski area, and finally descends back down to the village beside the Day Lodge. This loop is 5.8 km in length, with an elevation gain of 170 m. From this main loop, other trails branch off to other regions of the meadows. Quick access to the middle portion of the main loop can be obtained by taking the Standish Chairlift to the viewing platform. Do this early in the day before the build-up of tourists makes birding difficult. Rosy Finches often forage on the rocky ground beneath the lift. A short trail links the viewing platform with the main loop; White-tailed Ptarmigan and Prairie Falcon have been seen in this area.

After leaving the village, the main trail passes through the upper zone of the subalpine forest. In this area watch and listen for Townsend's

Solitaire; Hermit Thrush; Fox, Golden-crowned, and White-crowned Sparrows; and Dark-eyed Junco. Leaving behind the last tree islands the visitor enters the extensive alpine meadows. These meadows are not as productive as the treed areas for birds; however they offer great views of the surrounding mountains as well as a beautiful display of alpine flowers which reach their peak in mid-July. Horned Lark, Mountain Bluebird, American Pipit and Rosy Finch occur in these open areas. Overhead an occasional Northern Harrier, Swainson's Hawk, Red-tailed Hawk or Golden Eagle may be observed.

The water bodies of Rock Isle, Laryx and Grizzly Lakes as well as the ponds along the Twin Cairns segment of the main loop attract a few waterfowl and shorebirds. Reports of Common Loon, Common Merganser, Semipalmated Plover, Solitary Sandpiper and Spotted Sandpiper have come from these areas. The **Laryx-Grizzly Lake Loop** (4.4 km, 102 m elevation gain) is highly recommended. Watch and listen for Mountain and Boreal Chickadees; Red-breasted Nuthatch; and Yellow-rumped, Townsend's, and Wilson's Warblers during early July. This area is active again during the last two weeks of August and early September, when small mixed flocks migrate through it.

From the intersection with the Laryx-Grizzly loop the main trail climbs to meet the Standish connection and then passes behind the ski area into more alpine terrain. American Pipits can be seen performing their courtship displays in this area from early to mid-July. Large flocks of these birds occur during fall migration; Sharp-shinned Hawk, Cooper's Hawk and Merlin, which pass through this area in low numbers, are attracted to these flocks. Peregrine Falcons have been sighted on rare occasions during migration.

White-tailed Ptarmigan may be seen, with luck, in rocky meadows along the Twin Cairns segment of the trail, in the Quartz Ridge area, or around the edge of the Sunshine Meadows along the Simpson Pass trail. An intermediate level cross-country ski trip to the low summit of Quartz Ridge could be rewarded with a view of these elusive birds in winter plumage. From the connection with the Simpson Pass trail the main trail starts its descent to the village. On the way down there is the possibility of hearing Brewer's Sparrow singing as one begins to enter the trees. As the trail enters the more heavily forested area watch for both Golden and Ruby-crowned Kinglets, Varied Thrush, Pine Grosbeak, White-winged Crossbill and Pine Siskin.

More than 60 species of birds have been recorded at Sunshine; on a good day expect to find 20 or more species. Birding is hampered somewhat by the requirement to stay on the trails; this is very necessary, however, to protect the fragile meadows. Because of the elevation (2100–2400 metres), those not used to hiking at altitude may find the walking more taxing than normal. Also, those sensitive to the sun should consider using sunblock cream, hat and sunglasses. Alpine areas can experience severe storms, including snow, during the summer months. Always carry warm clothing while hiking in the meadows. During electrical storms the Gondola and Standish lifts are shut down. Expect long delays as other transportation is arranged, or walk down. Meals can be obtained at Sunshine Village but it is wise to pack a bag lunch.

JOHN McFAUL

D-6 The Lake Louise Area

The big attraction of the Lake Louise area is the magnificent scenery—you will probably not be inundated with birds. However, there are certainly interesting birds to be found, and this write-up describes two easily-accessible (and very scenic) half day birdwalks. There are many other trails in the same area, and a map is available from the park information service.

Drive to the Lake Louise exit on Hwy 1 in Banff National Park, about 170 km west of Calgary (2 hours driving time, non-stop). Follow the directional signs through Lake Louise Village to Lake Louise itself, 5 or 6 km from the exit. Birds to watch for while driving between Banff and Lake Louise are Harlequin Duck (summer) and American Dipper along the Bow River (dippers are often seen in winter, bobbing at the edge of the ice along open stretches of the river in the last 10 or 15 km before the Lake Louise exit), and perhaps a Steller's Jay (very uncommon).

Lake Louise: Plain of Six Glaciers Trail
This trail begins in front of Chateau Lake Louise. The first two and a half kilometres are flat and easy walking along the shore to a point

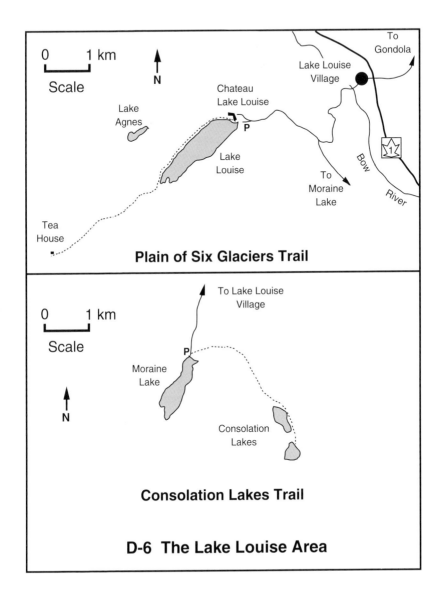

Plain of Six Glaciers Trail

Consolation Lakes Trail

D-6 The Lake Louise Area

slightly beyond the end of the lake, providing access to birds of the subalpine forest. Most, if not all, bird species to be expected can be found along this stretch. The next 3 km are moderately steep through glacial moraine, ending at the Plain of Six Glaciers Teahouse and spectacular views of Mt Victoria and surroundings. Sturdy footwear is recommended for this second section. The non-stop walking time from the Chateau to the end of the lake and back is about an hour to an hour and a half, but it is best to allow 3 hours or more to give adequate time for birding. Add another 3 hours to this if you wish to continue to the teahouse.

Birding is best during June and early July, when the snow has melted along the lake and the breeding birds are singing. However, many of the species are still around (but quieter) later in the summer, and some, such as Three-toed Woodpecker, Gray Jay, Steller's Jay, Clark's Nutcracker, Common Raven and Mountain Chickadee, can stay all winter. The best time of day is early to mid-morning, before the crowds build up.

Birds to be seen around the parking lot and hotel buildings include Gray Jay, Clark's Nutcracker, American Crow, Common Raven, American Robin and sometimes, Varied Thrush (check the lawns around the Chateau). A colony of Cliff Swallows nests on the Chateau. Violet-green and Barn Swallows used to nest there as well, but the recent renovations to the Chateau seem to have eliminated them; perhaps they will return. Along the lakeshore watch for Fox Sparrow near the canoe dock and buildings.

Just past the Chateau, there is a trail junction marked by a post with directional signs. Follow the left-hand branch (the trail to the Plain of Six Glaciers Teahouse) for 2 km along the shore to the end of the lake. Birds to be expected on a morning's walk through the forest along this stretch during the breeding season include Mountain Chickadee; Red-breasted Nuthatch; Winter Wren (listen for a long, bubbly song alternating between two pitches); both kinglets; Varied Thrush (a single drawn-out note, reminiscent of a telephone ringing, repeated on different pitches); Yellow-rumped Warbler; Townsend's Warbler (usually high in the trees; listen for a thin, relatively high-pitched song: se-se–se–SEE–see); and Pine Siskin.

Shortly before the end of the lake there is a brushy slope swept almost clear of trees by winter avalanches (no danger in summer). At this point the habitat changes from deep to open forest, gravel flats and cliffs. The trail runs up a small hill, then descends back to the lake level for a while before starting the ascent to the teahouse. Birds to listen and watch for along this section include Sharp-shinned Hawk (occasionally, near the cliffs); Olive-sided Flycatcher (quick-three–beers); Western Flycatcher (in the trees near the cliffs; soft, whistled song, "whee-weet", reminiscent of someone whistling for a dog); Winter Wren; Wilson's Warbler (usually in the shrubs near the water; often near the canoe dock); and Fox Sparrow (in the trees on or near the avalanche slope; listen for a loud song with slurred notes). As you climb higher towards the Teahouse you should also add Hermit Thrush.

Mammals to watch for on the hike are Least Chipmunk (striped, including the face); Golden-mantled Ground Squirrel (like an over-grown chipmunk, but lacks stripes on the face); Columbian Ground Squirrel (no stripes at all); Porcupine; Pika (in rockpiles; smaller than a ground squirrel; no tail); Hoary Marmot (also in rockpiles; size of a large housecat; bushy tail) and, possibly, Mountain Goat high up on the slopes.

Meals can be obtained at Chateau Lake Louise and snacks are available at the Teahouse during the summer tourist season. There are good washrooms at the parking lot, and outhouses at the Teahouse. Full tourist services are available in Lake Louise Village.

Moraine Lake: Consolation Lakes Trail
Follow the route description to Lake Louise, but about a kilometre before Lake Louise itself turn left at the directional sign for Moraine Lake. Drive 11 km to the parking lot at the end of this road.

The Consolation Lakes Trail starts from the large rockpile at the left-hand end of Moraine Lake (as seen from the parking lot). The trail runs through subalpine forest for about 3 km, mostly uphill but not steep, then opens out into rocks, open slopes and nice views at the first lake. The trail is good, but there is rock-hopping for the last hundred metres to the shore of the lake; good footwear is recommended. Allow half a day.

A walk in early August produced the following birds in the open forest and small meadows in the last half kilometre before the first lake: Mountain Chickadee, Red-breasted Nuthatch, both kinglets, Yellow-rumped Warbler, Fox Sparrow, White-winged Crossbill and Pine Siskin; and, on the rocks and along the stream where the trail reaches the first lake: Spotted Sandpiper, a migrating Solitary Sandpiper, Gray Jay, Clark's Nutcracker, half a dozen Townsend's Solitaires hawking insects from the rocks, Dark-eyed (Oregon) Junco and Pine Siskin. Varied Thrush and Pine Grosbeak have also been reported along the trail.

There are no facilities at the lakes. Good pit toilets are available at the Moraine Lake parking lot.

WILLIAM J.F. WILSON

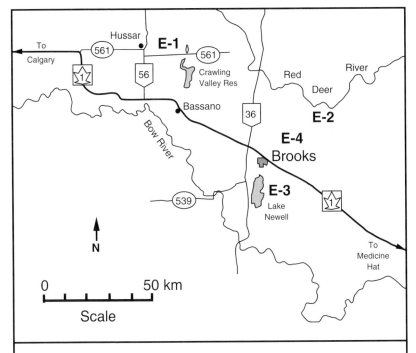

Section E: Brooks and the Eastern
Irrigation District

E-1   Wolf Lake and Crawling Valley Reservoir
E-2   Dinosaur Provincial Park
E-3   Kinbrook Island Provincial Park and Lake Newell
E-4   The Brooks Area

E-1 Wolf Lake and
Crawling Valley Reservoir

Wolf Lake is a large, shallow slough located about 110 km east of
Calgary on S.R. 561 while Crawling Valley Reservoir, to the south of
Wolf Lake, is one of the Eastern Irrigation District's major water bodies. They can be excellent for waterfowl and shorebirds during the
migration periods and for grassland species during the nesting season.
The round trip distance from Calgary city limits is about 260 km; a full
day will be required.

To reach **Wolf Lake** from Calgary, drive east on the Trans-Canada
Highway (Hwy 1) and turn left onto S.R. 561. This intersection is
about 22 km east of the town of Strathmore. Continue east on S.R. 561
for 27 km to Hussar. About 2 km east of Hussar turn right (south) on
Hwy 56 for 3.3 km, then left (east) onto S.R. 561 again. From this point
the road is gravel-surfaced and can be dusty when dry and very slippery when wet. Wolf Lake is reached after a further 23 km. Watch for
Merlin and Loggerhead Shrike in or near shelterbelts along this section. Wolf Lake stretches on both sides of the road and it is worthwhile scoping the shore and water from here, particularly during May,
late July, August and September when the shorebirds are migrating.
The eastern shore of the lake can be accessed by continuing 1.6 km east
and then turning north on a minor gravel road. There is an old "No
Trespassing" sign on the fence at this point but public access is permitted to these E.I.D. grasslands. Caution: this should be attempted only
if driving conditions are good.

During the nesting season, common birds on the lake include Eared
Grebe, Double-crested Cormorant, a variety of waterfowl and
American Coot. Great Blue Heron, Black-crowned Night-Heron,
Killdeer, American Avocet, Willet, Marbled Godwit and Wilson's
Phalarope can be seen along the shoreline. A walk through the grass-
lands surrounding the lake can produce Long-billed Curlew, Burrow-
ing Owl, Sprague's Pipit and McCown's Longspur as well as
abundant nesting populations of Horned Lark, Chestnut-collared
Longspur and Western Meadowlark. Overhead, watch for Northern
Harrier, Swainson's Hawk, Ferruginous Hawk, Golden Eagle and
Prairie Falcon.

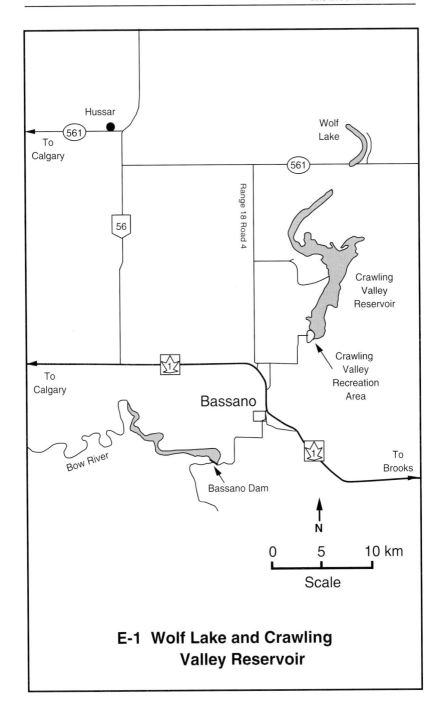

**E-1 Wolf Lake and Crawling
Valley Reservoir**

During spring and fall migration, Wolf Lake can be an excellent area for shorebirds and waterfowl. Tundra Swan, Greater White-fronted Goose, Snow Goose, Black-bellied Plover, Lesser Golden-Plover, yellowlegs, Hudsonian Godwit, Pectoral Sandpiper, Stilt Sandpiper, peeps, dowitchers, and Bonaparte's Gull have all been regularly recorded. Sharp-shinned and Cooper's Hawks as well as Peregrine Falcon are occasionally reported during the migration periods.

To visit the northern end of **Crawling Valley Reservoir** after birding Wolf Lake, start at the junction of the road along the east side of Wolf Lake and S.R. 561. Drive west on S.R. 561 for 11.3 km, then turn left (south) on Range 18 Road 4; this intersection is also marked by a small green sign for Bassano and Hwy 1. Continue south for 9.6 km and then turn left (east). You will recognize this intersection by a large red painted rock and an E.I.D. sign. Drive east for 3.5 km to a minor junction, take the right (southeast) fork and continue until you reach the reservoir, a distance of approximately 4.5 km. The road deteriorates to a single lane track, but it should present no problems if the surface is dry.

The birds in the grasslands adjacent to the reservoir are similar to those discussed earlier for Wolf Lake, but they can be more easily observed here. The reservoir also has birds similar to Wolf Lake, but because it is much larger and deeper, species such as Common Loon, Red-necked Grebe, American White Pelican, Double-crested Cormorant and a variety of diving ducks and gulls are more prevalent. There are nesting colonies of Double-crested Cormorant, Ring-billed Gull, California Gull and Common Tern on islands in the reservoir. The numbers and varieties of shorebirds, however, are not as great as at Wolf Lake.

If you do not wish to return the way you came when leaving the northern end of Crawling Valley Reservoir, turn left (south) on the major north-south gravel road with the red rock at the intersection. You will reach Hwy 1 near Bassano after about 10 km.

The southern end of the reservoir can be accessed at the **Crawling Valley Recreation Area**. This is reached from Hwy 1 by turning north just west of Bassano. The road immediately swings east and this should be followed for 5 km, then go north for 3 km, and finally east again for 2 km. The route is well sign-posted. There is more disturbance at the southern end of the reservoir as it is popular with boaters and fishermen, but it can be worth a visit during the waterfowl and shorebird migration periods.

If you have some time to spare at Bassano, a potentially good but under-birded location is **Bassano Dam** on the Bow River. The impressive setting alone is worth a visit. From the eastern access road, watch for a minor road crossing the railway tracks on the southern edge of town. This is marked by a small white directional sign with black letters. Follow the gravel road for 9 km to the dam. This can be a good location in May, and foraging flocks of American White Pelicans can be seen here during the summer.

There are no facilities at Wolf Lake or the northern end of Crawling Valley Reservoir. Crawling Valley Recreation Area has treated tap water and pit toilets. Gas can be obtained at Hussar. Full tourist facilities are available in Bassano and Strathmore.

HAROLD W. PINEL

E-2 Dinosaur Provincial Park

From Calgary, Dinosaur Provincial Park is approximately 3 hours and 230 km away by car. The park is reached by turning north off the Trans-Canada Highway at the Brooks overpass onto S.R. 873. This exit is clearly sign-posted as is the subsequent route, which follows S.R. 873, 544 and 551 north, east, then north again to the park entrance, past the hamlet of Patricia. The distance from the Trans-Canada Highway to the park entrance is 44 km. Dinosaur Provincial Park is suitable for a day of birding from Calgary, or could be combined with visits to nearby Lake Newell (E-3) and other locations in the Brooks area (E-4) on a two-day excursion.

Set in the Red Deer River badlands, Dinosaur Provincial Park encompasses a total area of 6,022 hectares. The park was designated a World Heritage Site in 1979 in recognition of both its rich palaeontological deposits and its scenic and wilderness resources. The extensive badlands found in the park were formed during the final stages of

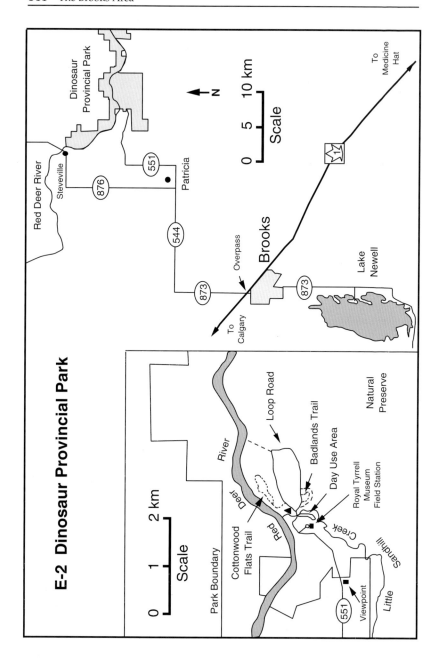

E-2 Dinosaur Provincial Park

glaciation. Differential erosion of sandstones and shales has resulted in dramatic badland features such as buttes, mesas, hoodoos and pipes, as well as the exposure of many Cretaceous fossils. Within the park, the Red Deer River is flanked by a 14 km stretch of relatively undisturbed riverine forest, containing dense stands of Plains Cotton-woods. Mixed grasslands are also found in the park, mostly on the prairie level around the perimeter. With such a diverse collection of landforms and habitats, Dinosaur Provincial Park is extremely reward-ing for birders. It offers a great variety and abundance of birds in a relatively small and easily accessible area.

Badlands cover approximately 75 percent of the park and support a unique bird fauna. Common badlands species include Say's Phoebe, Rock Wren, Mountain Bluebird and Lark Sparrow. Large Cliff Swallow colonies are common, with some colonies containing more than 30 nests. Violet-green Swallows are often found nesting in associ-ation with the Cliff Swallows. Several raptor species nest in the bad-lands. Prairie Falcons are quite common, nesting on cliffs and in piping channels. In 1988, four active Golden Eagle nests were found within the park; the eagles are frequently seen hunting over the prairie and badlands. Although there are more than 150 old Ferruginous Hawk nests in Dinosaur Provincial Park, only two active ones have been found recently. The Golden Eagles and Prairie Falcons generally over-winter in the park and are joined by one or two pairs of Bald Eagles.

The Red Deer River floodplain covers approximately 15 percent of the park and supports an extremely diverse and abundant bird fauna. Some of the highest breeding bird densities in Canada have been found in these cottonwood forests. The dawn chorus amongst the cottonwoods in the campground is definitely worth waking up for! American Kestrel, Common Nighthawk, Western Wood-Pewee, Gray Catbird, Brown Thrasher, Warbling Vireo, Rufous-sided Towhee and Northern Oriole are just a few of the species that a birder can be rewarded with after only a short time on the floodplain. Loggerhead Shrike and Yellow-breasted Chat occasionally nest where there is a dense tangle of Thorny Buffaloberry bushes. Northern Mockingbird has occasionally been sighted in the cottonwood forest, but no evi-dence of breeding has been found to date. In 1989 a pair of Pileated Woodpeckers nested in a cottonwood, close to the park campground. The floodplain is also an excellent area for migrants such as Orange-crowned, Blackpoll, and Black-and–white Warblers; American

Redstart; Rose-breasted Grosbeak; and White-throated Sparrow. Further away from the river, extensive areas of tall sagebrush are inhabited by Clay-colored, Brewer's (occasionally), and Vesper Sparrows, and Western Meadowlark.

Mixed-grass prairie surrounds Dinosaur Provincial Park and covers approximately 10 percent of the park. Northern Harrier, Long-billed Curlew, Horned Lark, Vesper Sparrow and Western Meadowlark are some of the species that are frequently sighted on the prairie. Less commonly seen are Ferruginous Hawk, Marbled Godwit, Loggerhead Shrike, Brewer's Sparrow and Lark Bunting. In winter, large flocks of Snow Buntings are common and Snowy Owls have been seen around the boundaries of the park.

The park campground, day-use area and Royal Tyrrell Museum Field Station are located on the south side of the Red Deer River. Much of Dinosaur Provincial Park is designated a "natural preserve" and cannot be entered except on a guided tour. However, there are a number of areas that can be easily accessed. Several hiking trails exist, beginning from the day-use and campground areas. These trails allow visitors to explore all of the main habitat types found within the park. Also, a 3.2 km loop road with fossil displays, can be walked or driven through the badlands and along the edge of the floodplain; two self-guiding trails lead off this loop road. The **Badlands Trail** is 1.5 km long and winds through some spectacular scenery. The **Cottonwood Flats Trail** is 1.6 km long and cuts across to the Red Deer River through sagebrush flats and cottonwood forest. As this area of cottonwood forest is not part of the natural preserve, one is able to wander off the trail and deeper into the forest.

From the viewpoint at the park entrance, it is possible to hike along the prairie at the edge of the badlands, but the prairie habitat is perhaps best covered by car. Driving some of the numerous gravelled roads surrounding the park, such as S.R. 876 can yield many prairie species, including raptors such as Ferruginous and Swainson's Hawks. Isolated Thorny Buffaloberry bushes along the roadsides are good places to look for breeding Loggerhead Shrikes.

One of the most interesting walks to take is to follow Little Sandhill Creek south from the day-use area. Although the eastern side of the creek is in the natural preserve, the western side is accessible to the public and supports a large variety of birds, ranging from badlands species such as Prairie Falcon, Rock Wren and Lark Sparrow to birds which favour the dense Thorny Buffaloberry thickets found along the creek, such as Yellow-breasted Chat, Gray Catbird and Brown Thrasher. If you have only a short amount of time to spend in the park, this route is one of the most rewarding.

The north side of the Red Deer River is accessible by following gravelled roads and crossing the Steveville bridge (see map). However, the park on the north side of the river can only be accessed by traversing private or leased land. Permission to enter the park by this route must be obtained from the landowners.

Sturdy footwear is recommended when hiking in the badlands because of the rugged terrain and, more importantly, the abundant prickly pear and pincushion cacti! Rattlesnakes are occasionally encountered; they are quite common in the Steveville area. If a rattlesnake is encountered, the best defence is to remain still until the snake moves away. During July and August the mosquito population is considerable, especially on the floodplain—insect repellent is highly recommended!

When visiting the park in summer, perhaps the most hazardous feature is the temperature. Temperatures in the river valley are generally higher than on the surrounding prairie due to the reflection of sunlight from the white badland surfaces. It is not uncommon to experience temperatures of 40°C (104°F) or higher. A hat and a good supply of drinking water are essential, even on very short walks.

Birders should use caution when birding in Dinosaur Provincial Park because of the susceptibility of breeding raptors to human disturbance. Ferruginous Hawks are listed as a threatened species in Canada and are particularly susceptible; they will readily abandon their nests if disturbed whilst incubating. In general, raptors should be watched from a distance, using a telescope.

The Dinosaur Provincial Park campground has 30 unserviced sites; there are pit toilets but no showers. Flush toilets are available in the nearby Royal Tyrrell Museum Field Station. A day-use picnic area is located next to Little Sandhill Creek. Interpretive programs and tours are offered from May to October. On the north side of the Steveville

Bridge is a small, unserviced campground. No registration or fee is required for this campsite; it has pit toilets, but no running water.

Gas, food and lodgings can be obtained in Patricia, 16 km southwest of the park. Full tourist facilities are available in Brooks.

ELIZABETH SAVOY

E-3 Kinbrook Island Provincial Park and Lake Newell

Kinbrook Island Provincial Park is situated on the eastern shore of Lake Newell and is approximately 200 km southeast of Calgary by road. After travelling east on the Trans-Canada Highway to Brooks, turn south on S.R. 873. The park is sign-posted at this exit. Drive south on S.R. 873 for 13 km, then turn right (west) onto the park access road. When visiting the park for the day, drive past the campground registration booth, take the first turn on the left and park in the visitors' parking lot. If camping in the park, the southern campground sections are much better for birds.

The park is relatively small. The overall impression is of a developed island with parking lots, beach areas, campgrounds and cottages. There are large lawn areas with ornamental trees and shrubs, especially in the campground and cottage areas. Native trees and shrubs, particularly willows, form peripheral vegetation in some areas. The island is bounded on the east by a marsh complex containing areas of open water, dense cattail and bulrush beds, mudflats, grassy areas and clumps of willow. The park access road bisects this marsh complex on a causeway. The remaining shoreline looks out over large expanses of Lake Newell.

Birding can be productive from April to November when there is open water, but the greatest diversity occurs between May and September. At this time, in addition to species inhabiting the aquatic environments, a number of summer resident passerines are found in the wooded areas of the island. The lawn and wooded areas near the

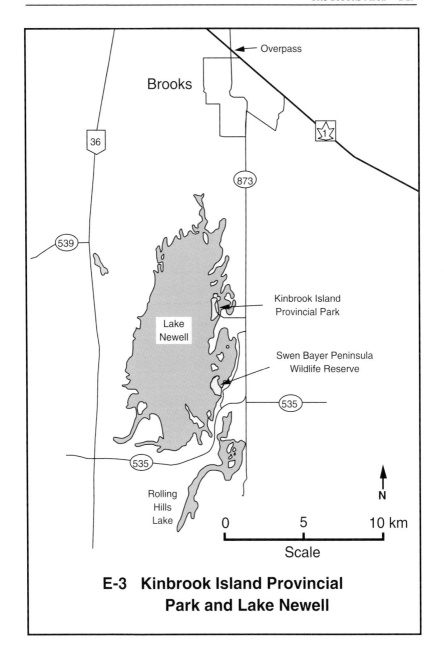

**E-3   Kinbrook Island Provincial
Park and Lake Newell**

campgrounds and cottages are best birded in the morning. Avoid weekends, if possible, during the summer months.

Common summer residents in the wooded areas include: Mourning Dove, Western Wood-Pewee, Least Flycatcher, Western Kingbird, Eastern Kingbird, House Wren, Cedar Waxwing, Warbling Vireo, Yellow Warbler, Common Grackle, Brown-headed Cowbird, Northern Oriole and American Goldfinch. Large numbers of Red-winged and Yellow-headed Blackbirds feed on the lawn areas and amongst the trees. During migration the trees on the island act as an oasis surrounded by grasslands and water. Species drawn to the park at these times have included Purple Martin, Red-breasted Nuthatch, Ruby-crowned Kinglet, Veery, Swainson's Thrush, Yellow-rumped Warbler, Blackpoll Warbler, American Redstart, and White-throated Sparrow.

Looking over the open expanses of Lake Newell during the summer, the birds most frequently observed are American White Pelican; Double-crested Cormorant; Franklin's, Ring-billed and California Gulls; and Common Tern. During migration, rafts of geese and ducks can be seen on the lake, as well as Common Loon and Horned, Red-necked, Eared and Western Grebes.

A number of species nest in the marsh complex including Pied-billed, Horned and Red-necked Grebes; Canada Goose; a variety of ducks; Northern Harrier; Sora; American Coot; Killdeer; Spotted Sandpiper; Common Snipe; Wilson's Phalarope; Black Tern; Marsh Wren; Common Yellowthroat; and Red-winged and Yellow-headed Blackbirds. Some birds such as Great Blue Heron and Black-crowned Night-Heron feed in the marshes and then fly back to their colonies. Willet, Long-billed Curlew and Marbled Godwit breed in the adjacent native grasslands and also feed in the marshes. During spring and fall migrations a variety of shorebirds are attracted to the marsh complex.

After birding at Kinbrook Island, an alternative to returning the way you came is to continue south on S.R. 873 (gravel-surfaced). If road conditions are good, turn right after 1.8 km onto a minor gravel road. McCown's Longspur has occurred in this area. The road parallels the shoreline, allowing further views of the lake and some of the islands. The **Swen Bayer Peninsula Wildlife Reserve** is reached at 5.3 km. Species to be expected in this small area of trees, shrubs and marsh are similar to those at Kinbrook Island; the passerine migration can be

excellent here in May. The road joins S.R. 535 after 7.4 km. (When
S.R. 873 turns west it becomes S.R. 535). Several dirt roads head north
across the grasslands from S.R. 535, giving access to parts of the southern shoreline. Continue west on S.R. 535 until Hwy 36 (paved) is
reached. Go north on Hwy 36 for 24 km to reach the Trans-Canada
Highway. This optional route, especially the gravel road sections,
allows you to drive slowly and scan the adjacent grasslands for
species such as Ferruginous Hawk, Burrowing Owl, Horned Lark, and
McCown's and Chestnut-collared Longspurs. Mammals that you may
see include Coyote, American Badger, White-tailed Prairie Hare,
Richardson's Ground Squirrel and Pronghorn.

Kinbrook Island Provincial Park has pit toilets and a concession serving snack foods during the summer months. Gas and meals can be
obtained at the junction of S.R. 535 and Hwy 36. Full tourist facilities
are available in the town of Brooks.

HAROLD W. PINEL

E-4 The Brooks Area

In the Brooks area, large tracts of grassland are privately owned by the
Eastern Irrigation District and, unless otherwise posted, can be
accessed for the purpose of activities such as birding. The E.I.D. has
prepared an excellent brochure, entitled the "Eastern Irrigation District
Wildlife Guide", and this can be obtained either from the Tourist
Information Bureau on the Trans-Canada Highway (open June-Aug),
or from the E.I.D. offices (located at 550 Industrial Rd, Brooks,
8.00 a.m. to 5.00 p.m. weekdays ; phone: 362–1400. Mailing address:
P.O. Bag 8, Brooks, Alberta, T0J 0J0). The Wildlife Guide consists of a
map showing the major features of the area, including the E.I.D. grasslands and water bodies and their access points. From a birder's point
of view it is more comprehensive and up-to–date than the topographic
maps and is extremely useful for birding this area thoroughly.
Grasslands are a very fragile ecosystem and it is important to use only
established roads and trails. Walk as much as possible rather than
driving as most access roads are dirt-surfaced and can be extremely

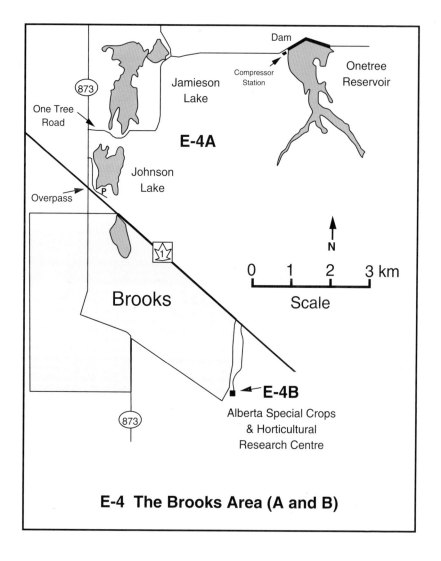

Dam

Compressor
Station

Onetree
Reservoir

873

Jamieson
Lake

One Tree
Road

E-4A

Johnson
Lake

Overpass

P

N

Brooks

0   1   2   3 km

Scale

E-4B

Alberta Special Crops
& Horticultural
Research Centre

873

E-4 The Brooks Area (A and B)

slippery and vulnerable to erosion in wet driving conditions. Use caution if range cattle are present as their behaviour can be unpredictable.

A. Onetree Reservoir Driving Route
This short route is suitable for birders with an hour or two to spare in Brooks and who would like to see some waterbirds and shorebirds, particularly during the migration periods. It can also be useful in early spring when deeper water bodies such as Lake Newell may still be frozen. The route begins at the junction of the Trans-Canada Highway and S.R. 873 (the major exit for downtown Brooks, hereafter called the "Brooks overpass"). Start driving north on S.R. 873 and immediately turn right at Johnson Lake (confusingly marked by a sign which says "Inter-Lake"). This fairly deep, cattail edged lake can be good for Common Loon, grebes, American White Pelican, Double-crested Cormorant, diving ducks, terns, Marsh Wren and Yellow-headed Blackbird. There is just enough room to park along the shore at the intersection **(km 0.0)**. For a safer view, continue for 0.7 km and park at the entrance to the pasture on the left.

Return to S.R. 873, turn right and drive north for 0.5 km, then turn right onto One Tree Road. In May, these irrigated fields may have Black-bellied Plover, and in August large flocks of Pine Siskins are attracted by the ripening small grain crops. At 2.8 and 3.3 kms the first bays of Jamieson Lake can be seen on the left. This large lake is edged with cattails, shrubs and natural grassland. Species will be similar to those found at Johnson Lake with the addition of more surface-feeding ducks. Western Kingbird can be common along the roadside in this section. As you continue, check any irrigated fields or muddy patches caused by leaking irrigation equipment for shorebirds. At 4 km a small marshy area on the right can be good in spring for shorebirds. At 5.3 km there is a closer view of Jamieson Lake. Check the shrubs on the far shore for roosting Black-crowned Night-Herons.

At the Y-junction turn left for a short distance to check out the lake from this angle. The cattail marsh on the right has Marsh Wren and Yellow-headed Blackbird. Turn round at the pull-out by the outlet canal and return to the Y-junction. Turn left and continue. The small slough on the right at 5.9 km is worth checking in spring. Continue past the "Dead End" sign at 7 km until Onetree Reservoir is reached, parking near the compressor station. In dry conditions, it is possible to drive the single lane track across the dam, turning your vehicle just beyond the second headworks. Large concentrations of waterbirds can occur on the reservoir during spring and fall. Check also the marshy area and exit canals on the other side of the dam for Black-crowned Night-Heron. Retrace the route for the return to Brooks.

B. Alberta Special Crops and Horticultural Research Centre

This research facility is situated on the south side of the Trans-Canada Highway, about 4.4 km east of the overpass in Brooks. The land-scaped grounds are open to the public at any time of day and, during the growing season, can be a welcome stop for anyone driving this part of the highway. It can be excellent for Blackpoll Warbler in May. In summer, check the formal flower beds for Ruby-throated Hum-mingbird. Common Grackle is easily seen here. The best time to visit, however, is in August when exceptional concentrations of migrating warblers and other small passerines can occur in the mature trees and shrubs around the buildings. These "fallouts" usually occur in the early morning following a late afternoon or evening thunderstorm. Have your insect repellent handy as the rise in humidity brings out the mosquitoes in full force.

C. Tillebrook Provincial Park

This campground is situated on the southern side of the Trans-Canada Highway, 8.6 km east of the overpass in Brooks. It makes an excellent centre for birders spending some days in the Brooks area as it has showers and electrical hook-ups, amenities lacking at both Kinbrook Island and Dinosaur Provincial Parks. Its well-watered grounds can be surprisingly birdy, particularly in May. Check the trees and shrubs for migrating flycatchers, thrushes, warblers and sparrows. A noisy nest-ing pair of Merlins is hard to miss. Towards dusk check the marshy grasslands to the south for Short-eared Owl. Burrowing Owl has nest-ed in the small patch of grassland between the park and the highway.

D. Hwy 36 South of the Trans-Canada Highway

This highway, 8 km west of Brooks, can be excellent for waterfowl and shorebirds during the migration periods, especially in May. It can also be very good for Snowy Owl in early and late winter. Distances are given from the Trans-Canada Highway to access points and do not include side trips.

Drive south on Hwy 36 for 17 km to the junction with S.R. 539. An area of shallow sloughs can be accessed by driving west on S.R. 539 for

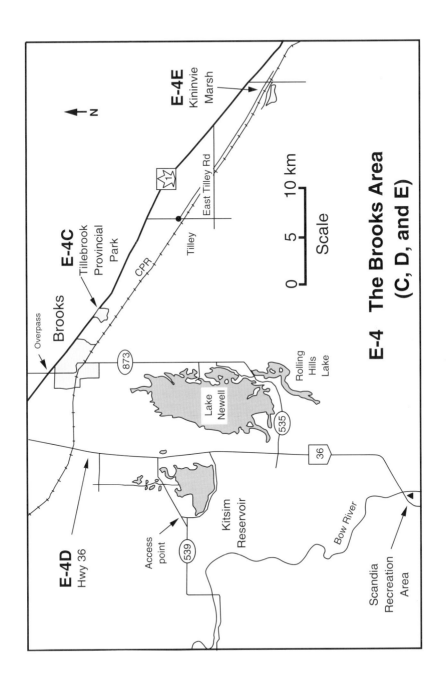

E-4 The Brooks Area (C, D, and E)

3 km and then turning north on a minor gravel road. This may be soft and rutted when wet. A series of variously sized sloughs stretches on either side of the road for the next 3.8 km. A male Garganey was photographed in the first slough beneath the powerline on May 18, 1991. The large slough on the right at 1.9 km has a well-developed cattail bed close to the road—check here for American Bittern. The northern-most slough on the right at about 3 km is the deepest and has more grebes and diving ducks. This slough may be viewed from a service road along the dam at the southern end. Check for Burrowing Owl whenever you have a good view of the grasslands.

Kitsim Reservoir is also accessed from S.R. 539. Opposite the road to the sloughs is a single lane track heading south across the grasslands. If this is ungated and in dry driving conditions, it can be followed for 2 km to the northern shore of the reservoir. The muddy shoreline at the northern end can be very good for shorebirds in May but the quantities of bugs stirred up as you walk the grassland can be a problem. The main access point for the reservoir is reached by continuing west on S.R. 539 for a further 4.2 km to the inlet canal. Turn left here onto the WEST bank of the canal. If the first section through the Texas gate is in poor condition, it may be advisable to continue west on S.R. 539 for a kilometre and make a sharp turn to the left onto a good gravel road. This joins the service road along the canal. The service road may be slowly driven for about 7 km around the western and south-ern shores of the reservoir. To access the grasslands, park by the dam and walk the gravel track beside the exit canal in the southwest corner. The reservoir is a good location for shorebirds in May and August; Ruddy Turnstone has been reported from rocky sections of the shore-line. The islands host breeding colonies of Double-crested Cormorant, Ring-billed and California Gulls, and Common Tern. Summer resi-dents of the grasslands include Burrowing Owl and McCown's Longspur. Prairie Falcon and Ferruginous Hawk may be seen over-head. Large numbers of Black-crowned Night-Herons have been observed feeding in the canal in the southwest corner in June and July. Watch for geese in September.

Continuing south of S.R. 539 on Hwy 36, the slough on the east side of the road at 18 km can be worth checking. Alberta's first Little Blue Heron was discovered here on May 19, 1991. The southern end of **Lake Newell** can be accessed by driving east on S.R. 535 (24 km). Large flocks of Black-bellied Plovers can occur along the shoreline during mid- to late May, together with the occasional Lesser Golden-Plover or Red Knot. Check here for geese in the fall.

Scandia Recreation Area is reached at 55 km. This small campground on the Bow River can be an excellent location for shorebirds during spring migration if water levels are correct; it has regularly produced Red Knot during the last three weeks of May. As you cross the river, slow down and watch for an inconspicuous gravel road on the left-hand side, marked by a small brown sign. The park provides access to about 150 m of shoreline east of the bridge. If no livestock are present, it is also possible to walk beneath the bridge to bird the western side—but please note that this is private property. In spring, a large part of the Bow River's flow is diverted into the E.I.D. irrigation system at Bassano, leaving the river downstream of the dam very shallow and exposing the muddy shoreline and many gravel bars. Good sized flocks of peeps can occur and Black-necked Stilt has been observed here. Large flocks of Black-bellied Plovers use the gravel bar west of the bridge as a resting area, and these should be methodically scoped for small numbers of Red Knots and the occasional Ruddy Turnstone. If there has been a particularly high spring runoff more water will be released from the dam, in which case Scandia will not be a good shorebird location at the critical time. To save yourself a wasted journey, check with the Bassano Dam Operator (phone: 641–2111) for information on the river's flow.

Gas and meals can be obtained at the junction of Hwy 36 and S.R. 535.

E. Finding McCown's Longspur

In Alberta, McCown's Longspur reaches its greatest abundance in the southeast corner of the province near Wildhorse. It is a moderately common, but local, breeder in the Brooks area. A reliable way to find this sought-after species is to drive the minor gravel roads off the Trans-Canada Highway through the arid grasslands east of Tilley. The most rewarding time to look for longspurs is when the males are performing their territorial song flights in late May and June. The song flights can also be an excellent way of separating McCown's from Chestnut-collared at a distance. The males of both species rise up into the air singing with rapidly beating wings. The McCown's male then immediately floats back down with his wings held stiffly above his back. The Chestnut-collared male prolongs his song flight in undulating circles, finally returning to his perch with still rapidly beating wings.

A good location where the quest for McCown's Longspur can be combined with a search for spring vagrants is **Kininvie Marsh**. This is reached by driving east on the Trans-Canada Highway from the Brooks overpass for 37.4 km and turning right (south) on a minor gravel road. There is no highway sign at this intersection but it can be recognized by a small powerline paralleling the road. (For westbound travellers, the Kininvie road is 27.9 km west of the intersection with S.R. 884 at Suffield.)   After driving south for 2 km an unmarked railway crossing is reached. Cross this single track with caution as it is the main line and quite busy. Immediately after crossing the railway, turn right onto a small gravel track. This lush wetland forms a startling contrast to the arid grassland surrounding it. During spring migration and the nesting season it can be teeming with birdlife. At the time of writing, the cattail beds host a large breeding colony of Franklin's Gulls and it can be a good location for American Bittern. Rarities recorded during May, 1992 include White-faced Ibis and Black-necked Stilt. McCown's Longspur can be abundant along the roadsides in this general area and Burrowing Owl is a good possibility.

There are no facilities at Kininvie. Gas, meals and washrooms are available in Tilley.

JOAN McDONALD

Species Locator

Red-throated Loon – Observed irregularly in fall on large water bodies such as Glenmore Reservoir (A-6) and Eagle Lake (B-3).

Pacific Loon – Observed infrequently (almost annually) in fall on large water bodies such as Glenmore Reservoir (A-6), Eagle Lake (B-3) and Namaka Lake (B-4). Other recent locations include Bruce Lake (B-6) and the Bow River in Calgary (A-1).

Clark's Grebe – Accidental in the Region but should be looked for carefully. Nearest breeding population is outside the Region at Crow Indian Lake, southeast of Lethbridge.

American White Pelican – Nests at Lake Newell (E-3) and several other locations in the Brooks area. Foraging flocks usually occur on major rivers and lakes southeast of Calgary, especially at Carseland Weir (B-1).

American Bittern – Elusive, more often heard than seen. Try the north end of Bruce Lake (B-6) and the north side of Namaka Lake (B-4).

Great, Snowy and Cattle Egrets – Accidental but ranges are expanding. To be looked for in the Region.

Black-crowned Night-Heron – Lakes and ponds with cattails, also irrigation ditches; especially Bruce Lake (B-6) and the Brooks area (E-3, E-4).

White-faced Ibis – Regularly sighted at Pakowki Lake in southeast Alberta since 1974. Breeds in northern Montana. Vagrant in the Calgary Region.

Trumpeter Swan – Migrates in small groups, generally west of Calgary. In spring try the pond at the junction of the Trans-Canada Highway and Jumping Pound Road (take the exit 22.7 km west of Canada Olympic Park; a good view of the pond can then be obtained from the on ramp), and the ponds at the junction of the Trans-Canada Highway and Sibbald Creek Trail (C-10).

GEESE – A major staging area for Greater White-fronted, Snow and Ross' Geese, during both spring and fall migrations, lies between Hanna (on the northeast boundary of the Calgary Region) and Kindersley in Saskatchewan. In the Calgary Region they occur as follows:

Greater White-fronted Goose – Most likely near Brooks (E-1, E-3, E-4D). In fall, also try Eagle (B-3) and Namaka (B-4) lakes.

Snow Goose – As previous species, but higher numbers pass through the Region. In fall, greatest concentration occurs at McGregor Lake (B-9) and to the east.

Ross' Goose – Occasionally occurs on major water bodies east of Calgary and on the Bow River.

Wood Duck – There is an introduced population at Inglewood Bird Sanctuary (A-1) but wild birds are found occasionally throughout the Region.

Cinnamon Teal – Fairly reliable on shallow water bodies east of Calgary.

Eurasian Wigeon – Reported in small but increasing numbers throughout the Region.

Greater Scaup – Probably annual in small numbers on larger water bodies but identification requires care. In Calgary in fall, it is worthwhile trying Glenmore Reservoir (A-6) and the Bow River (A-1, A-8).

Harlequin Duck – Breeds on the upper Highwood, Elbow and Sheep Rivers, and the Bow River in Banff National Park. Overwinters in very small numbers along the Bow River in Calgary, especially at the Inglewood Bird Sanctuary and near the Glenmore Trail Bridge (A-1, A-8).

Oldsquaw – Regular in very small numbers in fall, especially on Glenmore Reservoir (A-6); also on the Bow River, e.g. Carseland Weir (B-1).

Black Scoter – Occasional fall records from Glenmore Reservoir (A-6), Eagle Lake (B-3) and Barrier Lake (C-11).

Surf Scoter – Regular in small numbers. In spring on mountain lakes; in fall on Glenmore Reservoir (A-6), Eagle Lake (B-3) and at Seebe Pond (C-7).

Barrow's Goldeneye – Breeds on mountain lakes. Most easily found in winter along the Bow River in Calgary, especially at Carburn Park (A-8).

Hooded Merganser – Most easily seen on migration at the Inglewood Bird Sanctuary (A-1) and in winter on the Bow River near the Glenmore Trail Bridge (A-8).

Red-breasted Merganser – During spring migration most often seen at Bruce Lake and the Irricana sloughs (B-6). In spring and fall also on the Bow River in Calgary (A-1, A-8) and Glenmore Reservoir (A-6).

Turkey Vulture – Seen regularly in the Red Deer River valley, especially at Dry Island Buffalo Jump Provincial Park and in the Drumheller area (B-7).

Osprey – May be found along the Bow River in and west of Calgary. Nests at the first Vermilion Lake in Banff National Park (D-2).

Bald Eagle – A strong spring migration occurs through the foothills west of Calgary (C-2, C-4, C-5). Winters along the Bow River in Calgary (A-8).

Ferruginous Hawk – Nests sparsely east of Calgary. Most likely at Dinosaur Provincial Park (E-2) and along the Trans-Canada Highway east of Brooks. Becomes more numerous outside the Region in the general area northeast of Brooks.

Golden Eagle – Widespread but elusive. Most easily found during spring migration through the foothills with Bald Eagles (C-2, C-5, C-12) and especially in the Kananaskis (C-11).

Peregrine Falcon – Birds from breeding programs have nested on tall buildings in downtown Calgary since the early 1980s.

Gyrfalcon – Annual winter visitor reported with increasing frequency in the Calgary area (due perhaps to the abundance of overwintering ducks). Try along the Bow River (A-8); the Forest Lawn stormwater retention pond if ducks are present (B-5); Horse Creek Road (C-2); and Nose Hill (A-5).

Blue Grouse – Widespread but scarce in the higher foothills and mountains. Easiest to find at the Sheep River Sanctuary (C-5).

White-tailed Ptarmigan – Frustratingly elusive. In early summer try around the tops of the Lake Louise and Sunshine Meadows (D-5) gondolas; Bow Summit (can also be seen from the highway in winter) and Parker Ridge on the Icefields Parkway in Banff National Park; and Ptarmigan Cirque in the Highwood Pass (C-12). Your chances of finding them increase after the first snows in fall when their tracks may be followed.

Wild Turkey – Introduced in the Porcupine Hills south of the Region; may be spreading. Has been seen as far north as the Sheep River valley. More reliable at Cypress Hills Provincial Park, southeast of Medicine Hat.

SHOREBIRDS – Good locations vary from year to year depending on water body levels. Some good Spring Locations close to Calgary in recent years have been: Railway Slough near Irricana (B-6); Langdon Slough near the junction of the Trans-Canada Highway and Hwy 9 (B-6); Sadler's Slough (B-2); and Dawson Lake (10.4 km north of Strathmore on S.R. 817). Fall Locations are: Dalemead Reservoir (B-1); Johnson's Island (B-1); the east end of Namaka Lake (B-4); and the south end of Eagle Lake (B-3).

Piping Plover – Scarce in the Region. Possible at Hand Hills and Little Fish lakes (east of Drumheller).

Upland Sandpiper – Becoming very hard to find in the Region. Possible wherever there is unplowed native grassland that has not been overgrazed.

Red Phalarope – The only location in the Region where it has been recorded at all regularly is Namaka Lake (B-4) in late fall.

GULLS – During migration large numbers of gulls congregate at certain locations where it is possible to study them at close range. Inglewood Bird Sanctuary (A-1) is the most outstanding. Other good locations are: the southern end of Eagle Lake (B-3); the southeast corner of Namaka Lake (B-4); Carseland Weir (B-1); Carburn Park (A-8); and Lac Des Arcs (C-8).

Forster's Tern – In spring and summer present at Eagle (B-3), Namaka (B-4) and Bruce (B-6) lakes and in the Brooks area. Readily identified in September when fall-plumaged birds (together with Common Terns) feed at the southern end of Eagle Lake and Carseland Weir (B-1).

Snowy Owl – Can be found during most winters anywhere east of Calgary by slowly driving the side roads. Some of the most reliable areas near the city are: Shepard (B-1), Indus, Langdon, and around the airport.

Northern Hawk Owl – Irruptive. Most likely to be seen in winter along edges of mixed forest in the foothills; try along the Grand Valley Road to Water Valley area (C-2, C-3).

Northern Pygmy-Owl – Widely distributed in the foothills but numbers fluctuate from year to year.

Burrowing Owl – Has nested in pastureland east of Calgary; local in the Brooks area. Numbers have seriously declined recently—your best chance may be outside the Region in eastern Alberta.

Barred Owl – Elusive in heavy, mixed woodland. Has occurred regularly at the western end of Fish Creek Provincial Park (A-2).

Great Gray Owl – Most sightings have been in the Water Valley area (C-3) but can occur throughout the foothills. Somewhat irruptive.

Boreal Owl – Calls after dark on calm nights in March and April along the Sibbald Creek Trail (C-10).

Northern Saw-whet Owl – Very widely distributed in the foothills. Can be heard calling on calm nights in April, most reliably along the Sibbald Creek Trail (C-10), in the Water Valley area (C-3) and at Brown Lowery Recreation Area (C-6).

Common Nighthawk – Declining. Along river valleys, especially at Dinosaur Provincial Park (E-2). In Calgary try Inglewood (A-1).

Black Swift – Nests in Johnston Canyon (D-3) in Banff National Park.

Ruby-throated Hummingbird – Regularly nests on the valley bottom in the Weaselhead Natural Area (A-6) in Calgary; can also be found at the Alberta Special Crops and Horticultural Research Centre in Brooks (E-4).

Calliope Hummingbird – Most easily found until early July at moist locations in mountain valleys where males are on territory. Has been regular at Bow Valley Provincial Park (C-7) and Strawberry Campground marsh (C-12). Try also at feeders in Exshaw, Seebe and Highwood House (C-12).

Rufous Hummingbird – Widespread in the foothills. Good locations are: along the bluff in the north Weaselhead Natural Area (A-6); along the Many Springs Trail in Bow Valley Provincial Park (C-7); and along the Highwood Trail (S.R. 541) east of Highwood Junction (C-12).

Red-naped Sapsucker – Can be found in the foothills southwest of Calgary, particularly in the Sheep (C-5) and Highwood (C-12) valleys.

Three-toed Woodpecker – Widespread but elusive in coniferous woodlands in the foothills. Try Brown Lowery Recreation Area (C-6) or the Water Valley area (C-3). In Calgary has been found in Edworthy Park (A-3), and at the western end of Fish Creek Provincial Park (A-2). In Banff try the Fenland Trail (D-2).

Black-backed Woodpecker – Extremely hard to find in the Region. Found in similar habitat to the previous species but prefers recently burned areas. Brown Lowery (C-6) is the most likely location.

Willow Flycatcher – Much less widespread in the Region than Alder Flycatcher. Try the beaver pond on the Flowing Waters Trail in Bow Valley Provincial Park (C-7), and along Hwy 40 north of Highwood Junction (C-12).

Hammond's Flycatcher – Most easily found at the Muleshoe Picnic Area in Banff National Park (D-4).

Dusky Flycatcher – Can be found locally throughout the foothills. Try at deciduous stands along the Highwood Trail (S.R. 541) east of Highwood Junction (C-12), and the Many Springs Trail in Bow Valley Provincial Park (C-7).

The Western Flycatcher Complex - The recent split, based on the vocalizations of males, of the Western Flycatcher into **Cordilleran** and **Pacific-slope Flycatchers** is difficult to apply in the Region. Found in steep-sided river valleys in the foothills. Try William J. Bagnall Wilderness Park (formerly Silver Creek) (C-3), and the Sheep (C-5) and Highwood (C-12) rivers. In Calgary try the west end of Fish Creek Provincial Park (A-2).

Say's Phoebe – Most easily found during the nesting season in the Drumheller (B-7) and Dinosaur Provincial Park badlands (E-2).

Western Kingbird – Widely distributed east and south of Calgary; most easily found in the Brooks area.

Violet-green Swallow – Found at Grassi Lakes near Canmore (C-9), and along the Bow River at Seebe (C-7) and Banff. On the prairies try Dinosaur Provincial Park (E-2).

Clark's Nutcracker – Try around Canmore, Banff and Lake Louise. Widespread but sometimes scarce in winter.

Rock Wren – Try badlands in the Drumheller area (B-7) and in Dinosaur Provincial Park (E-2).

Winter Wren – Local in the mountains. Try Johnston Canyon (D-3) and the Bourgeau Lake Trail in Banff National Park, and King Creek Canyon in the Kananaskis Valley (C-11).

American Dipper – Try below the dam at Seebe (C-7), Johnston Canyon (D-3) in Banff National Park, and Elbow Falls (on Hwy 66 west of Bragg Creek).

Varied Thrush – In summer found in older, damp, coniferous forests close to the Continental Divide. During migration more widespread.

Sprague's Pipit – Found in moderately grazed grassland east of the foothills. From mid-May to late July, most often located by distinctive aerial song.

Loggerhead Shrike – Seldom seen away from short-grass prairie. Provincial stronghold is east of Dinosaur Provincial Park (E-2).

Solitary Vireo – Breeds in the mountains and foothills at such locations as the Sheep River valley (C-5), Brown Lowery Recreation Area (C-6) and the Water Valley area (C-3).

Philadelphia Vireo – In the early 1980s singing males occurred in the foothills west of Water Valley. Most likely to be encountered as a fall migrant, e.g. at the Inglewood Bird Sanctuary (A-1).

WARBLERS – The best locations within Calgary for observing migrant warblers are: Inglewood Bird Sanctuary (A-1), Pearce Estate Park (see map A-1), and Lowery Gardens (A-3). Warblers in the Region tend to fall into three groups:

Group A: Those which nest throughout the Region. This group consists of Yellow Warbler and Common Yellowthroat.

Group B: Those which nest only in the foothills and mountain portion of the Region but are found throughout on migration. This group consists of Tennessee, Orange-crowned, Yellow-rumped, Townsend's, American Redstart, Ovenbird, Northern Waterthrush, MacGillivray's, and Wilson's.

Townsend's Warbler – Uncommon summer resident of damp stands of tall spruce and fir in the mountains. Typically forages in tree tops—best located by its wheezy song. Try Johnston Canyon (D-3), Fenland Trail (D-2) and Lake Louise (D-6) in Banff National Park. Small numbers pass through Calgary (A-1, A-3) in fall migration.

Group C: Those which do not generally nest, but which might be found almost anywhere on migration. There are breeding records for the following four species:

Chestnut-sided Warbler – Has been found singing on territory near the beaver pond on the Flowing Waters Trail in Bow Valley Provincial

Park (C-7) and at the western end of Winchell Lake (C-3); an adult feeding one young was observed in the Weaselhead (A-6) in 1992.

Cape May Warbler – Was found singing on territory at Brown Lowery Recreation Area (C-6) in four summers in the early 1980s.

Connecticut Warbler – Territorial males have been reported from the Water Valley area since the mid-1980s.

Yellow-breasted Chat – Nests at Dinosaur Provincial Park (E-2).

Lazuli Bunting – Breeds on aspen-covered slopes in the foothills southwest of Calgary, particularly in the Highwood (C-12) and Sheep (C-5) valleys. It has occurred irregularly on Nose Hill (A-5).

Rufous-sided Towhee – Most easily found at locations in the Red Deer River valley such as Dinosaur Provincial Park (E-2), the Drumheller area (B-7), and Dry Island Buffalo Jump Provincial Park.

Brewer's Sparrow – The prairie subspecies occurs in Dinosaur Provincial Park (E-2), while the alpine subspecies breeds above timberline. Possible locations for the latter are: Sunshine Meadows (D-5) and the Highwood Pass (C-12).

Lark Sparrow – Restricted in the Region to the Red Deer River valley area, particularly Dinosaur Provincial Park (E-2).

Lark Bunting – In some years can be seen from the Trans-Canada Highway between Brooks and Medicine Hat. More commonly found southeast of the Region.

Baird's Sparrow – Some recent locations include: near the Irricana sloughs (B-6), Bruce Lake (B-6), Namaka Lake (B-4), and west of Little Fish Lake. Numbers vary considerably from year to year. To find this species learn its distinctive song.

Sharp-tailed Sparrow – This species' normal range is north of the Region but it has been found in a marsh complex near Big Hill Springs Provincial Park (C-1) since the late 1980s.

Fox Sparrow – Breeds close to timberline in the mountains. Good locations are: the Highwood Pass (C-12) and Sunshine Meadows (D-5).

Swamp Sparrow – Extremely local breeder west of the Forestry Trunk Road (S.R. 940), north of Hwy 1A. Small numbers pass through Calgary in fall migration—try areas of riverine shrubbery.

Golden-crowned Sparrow – Found in shrubby areas at timberline. An accessible and reliable location in Banff National Park is Parker Ridge, on the Icefields Parkway near the Jasper Park boundary. It has also been reported from the Bow Summit area, Sunshine Meadows (D-5) and the Lake Louise area.

McCown's Longspur – Prefers dry short-grass prairie. The most accessible location is east of Tilley, south of the Trans-Canada Highway (E-4E). In dry driving conditions try the east side of Wolf Lake (E-1) and the southeast side of Lake Newell (E-3).

Chestnut-collared Longspur – The common breeding longspur of the eastern half of the Region. Usually prefers denser, taller, short-grass prairie than McCown's. Good locations include the east and south sides of Lake Newell (E-3), the Tilley area (E-4E), and the eastern side of McGregor Lake (B-9).

Rosy Finch – In summer found in small groups on rocky slopes above tree line. Sunshine Meadows (D-5) is a likely location. Gathers into large flocks in fall, when they become more widespread at lower elevations.

Purple Finch – Found in mixed woodland in the foothills. In Calgary try the western end of Fish Creek Provincial Park (A-2) and the Weaselhead (A-6).

Seasonal Status
and Abundance Chart

The Seasonal Status and Abundance Chart has been designed to conservatively show the probability of finding species which regularly occur within the Calgary Region. This data has been generated from records published since 1975, augmented by the compilers' personal experience. Species which have been reported in fewer than five years since 1975 are listed separately in the Rarely-Observed Species list following the Chart. The Chart may also be used as a checklist.

The bar graphs do not represent absolute numbers, but rather your chances of finding a given species. It assumes that you are competent at identification and are in appropriate habitat. There are five categories of probability:

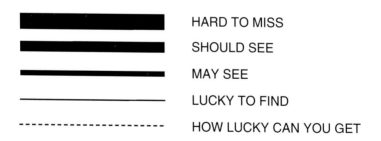

Species which are followed by the symbol "†" can be found in the Species Locator.

	Jan Feb Mar Apr May Jun Jul Aug Sep Oct Nov Dec
☐ Red-throated Loon [†]	
☐ Pacific Loon [†]	
☐ Common Loon	
☐ Pied-billed Grebe	
☐ Horned Grebe	
☐ Red-necked Grebe	
☐ Eared Grebe	
☐ Western Grebe	
☐ American White Pelican [†]	
☐ Double-crested Cormorant	
☐ American Bittern [†]	
☐ Great Blue Heron	
☐ Black-crowned Night-Heron [†]	
☐ White-faced Ibis [†]	
☐ Tundra Swan	
☐ Trumpeter Swan [†]	
☐ Greater White-fronted Goose [†]	
☐ Snow Goose [†]	
☐ Ross' Goose [†]	
☐ Canada Goose	
☐ Wood Duck [†]	
☐ Green-winged Teal	
☐ American Black Duck	
☐ Mallard	
☐ Northern Pintail	
☐ Blue-winged Teal	
☐ Cinnamon Teal [†]	
☐ Northern Shoveler	
	Jan Feb Mar Apr May Jun Jul Aug Sep Oct Nov Dec

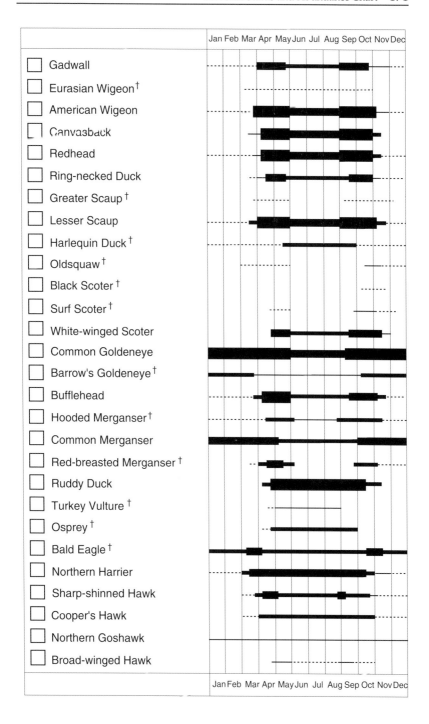

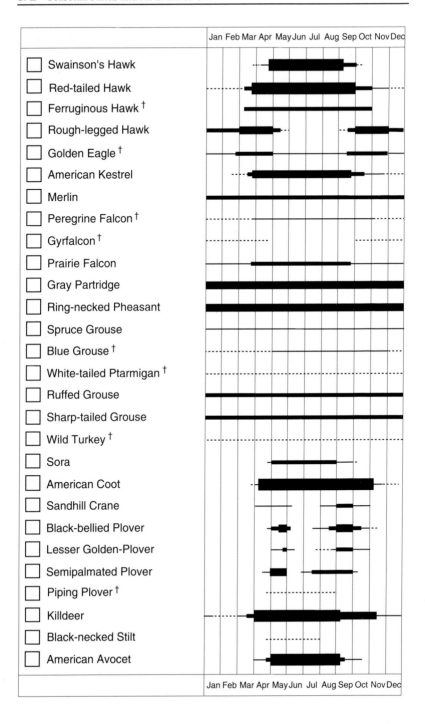

	Jan Feb Mar Apr May Jun Jul Aug Sep Oct Nov Dec
☐ Swainson's Hawk	
☐ Red-tailed Hawk	
☐ Ferruginous Hawk †	
☐ Rough-legged Hawk	
☐ Golden Eagle †	
☐ American Kestrel	
☐ Merlin	
☐ Peregrine Falcon †	
☐ Gyrfalcon †	
☐ Prairie Falcon	
☐ Gray Partridge	
☐ Ring-necked Pheasant	
☐ Spruce Grouse	
☐ Blue Grouse †	
☐ White-tailed Ptarmigan †	
☐ Ruffed Grouse	
☐ Sharp-tailed Grouse	
☐ Wild Turkey †	
☐ Sora	
☐ American Coot	
☐ Sandhill Crane	
☐ Black-bellied Plover	
☐ Lesser Golden-Plover	
☐ Semipalmated Plover	
☐ Piping Plover †	
☐ Killdeer	
☐ Black-necked Stilt	
☐ American Avocet	
	Jan Feb Mar Apr May Jun Jul Aug Sep Oct Nov Dec

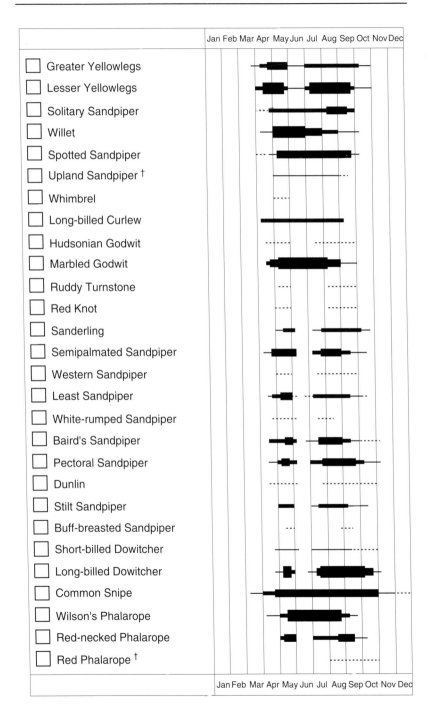

	Jan Feb Mar Apr May Jun Jul Aug Sep Oct Nov Dec
☐ Greater Yellowlegs	
☐ Lesser Yellowlegs	
☐ Solitary Sandpiper	
☐ Willet	
☐ Spotted Sandpiper	
☐ Upland Sandpiper †	
☐ Whimbrel	
☐ Long-billed Curlew	
☐ Hudsonian Godwit	
☐ Marbled Godwit	
☐ Ruddy Turnstone	
☐ Red Knot	
☐ Sanderling	
☐ Semipalmated Sandpiper	
☐ Western Sandpiper	
☐ Least Sandpiper	
☐ White-rumped Sandpiper	
☐ Baird's Sandpiper	
☐ Pectoral Sandpiper	
☐ Dunlin	
☐ Stilt Sandpiper	
☐ Buff-breasted Sandpiper	
☐ Short-billed Dowitcher	
☐ Long-billed Dowitcher	
☐ Common Snipe	
☐ Wilson's Phalarope	
☐ Red-necked Phalarope	
☐ Red Phalarope †	
	Jan Feb Mar Apr May Jun Jul Aug Sep Oct Nov Dec

	Jan	Feb	Mar	Apr	May	Jun	Jul	Aug	Sep	Oct	Nov	Dec
☐ Parasitic Jaeger												
☐ Franklin's Gull												
☐ Bonaparte's Gull												
☐ Mew Gull												
☐ Ring-billed Gull												
☐ California Gull												
☐ Herring Gull												
☐ Thayer's Gull												
☐ Glaucous-winged Gull												
☐ Glaucous Gull												
☐ Sabine's Gull												
☐ Caspian Tern												
☐ Common Tern												
☐ Forster's Tern †												
☐ Black Tern												
☐ Rock Dove												
☐ Band-tailed Pigeon												
☐ Mourning Dove												
☐ Great Horned Owl												
☐ Snowy Owl †												
☐ Northern Hawk Owl †												
☐ Northern Pygmy-Owl †												
☐ Burrowing Owl †												
☐ Barred Owl †												
☐ Great Gray Owl †												
☐ Long-eared Owl												
☐ Short-eared Owl												
☐ Boreal Owl †												
	Jan	Feb	Mar	Apr	May	Jun	Jul	Aug	Sep	Oct	Nov	Dec

Species	Jan	Feb	Mar	Apr	May	Jun	Jul	Aug	Sep	Oct	Nov	Dec
☐ Northern Saw-whet Owl †												
☐ Common Nighthawk †												
☐ Black Swift †												
☐ Ruby-throated Hummingbird †												
☐ Calliope Hummingbird †												
☐ Rufous Hummingbird †												
☐ Belted Kingfisher												
☐ Lewis' Woodpecker												
☐ Red-headed Woodpecker												
☐ Yellow-bellied Sapsucker												
☐ Red-naped Sapsucker †												
☐ Downy Woodpecker												
☐ Hairy Woodpecker												
☐ Three-toed Woodpecker †												
☐ Black-backed Woodpecker †												
☐ Northern Flicker												
☐ Pileated Woodpecker												
☐ Olive-sided Flycatcher												
☐ Western Wood-Pewee												
☐ Yellow-bellied Flycatcher												
☐ Alder Flycatcher												
☐ Willow Flycatcher †												
☐ Least Flycatcher												
☐ Hammond's Flycatcher †												
☐ Dusky Flycatcher †												
☐ "Western" Flycatcher †												
☐ Eastern Phoebe												
☐ Say's Phoebe †												

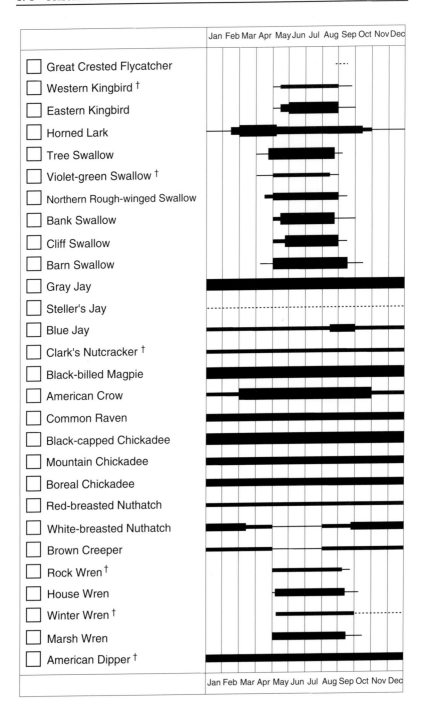

	Jan Feb Mar Apr May Jun Jul Aug Sep Oct Nov Dec
☐ Great Crested Flycatcher	
☐ Western Kingbird †	
☐ Eastern Kingbird	
☐ Horned Lark	
☐ Tree Swallow	
☐ Violet-green Swallow †	
☐ Northern Rough-winged Swallow	
☐ Bank Swallow	
☐ Cliff Swallow	
☐ Barn Swallow	
☐ Gray Jay	
☐ Steller's Jay	
☐ Blue Jay	
☐ Clark's Nutcracker †	
☐ Black-billed Magpie	
☐ American Crow	
☐ Common Raven	
☐ Black-capped Chickadee	
☐ Mountain Chickadee	
☐ Boreal Chickadee	
☐ Red-breasted Nuthatch	
☐ White-breasted Nuthatch	
☐ Brown Creeper	
☐ Rock Wren †	
☐ House Wren	
☐ Winter Wren †	
☐ Marsh Wren	
☐ American Dipper †	
	Jan Feb Mar Apr May Jun Jul Aug Sep Oct Nov Dec

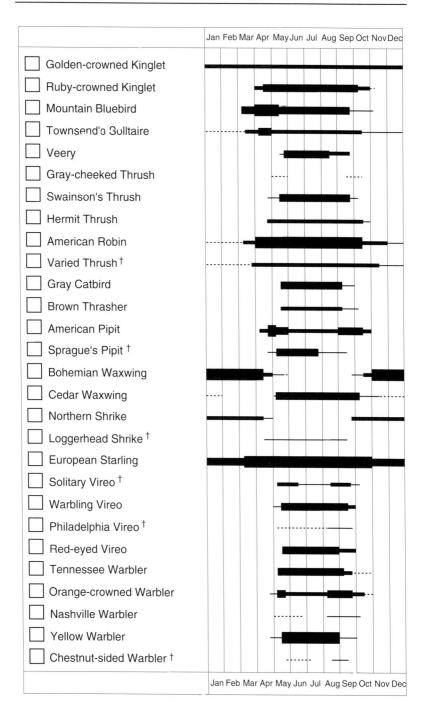

	Jan Feb Mar Apr May Jun Jul Aug Sep Oct Nov Dec
☐ Golden-crowned Kinglet	
☐ Ruby-crowned Kinglet	
☐ Mountain Bluebird	
☐ Townsend's Solitaire	
☐ Veery	
☐ Gray-cheeked Thrush	
☐ Swainson's Thrush	
☐ Hermit Thrush	
☐ American Robin	
☐ Varied Thrush †	
☐ Gray Catbird	
☐ Brown Thrasher	
☐ American Pipit	
☐ Sprague's Pipit †	
☐ Bohemian Waxwing	
☐ Cedar Waxwing	
☐ Northern Shrike	
☐ Loggerhead Shrike †	
☐ European Starling	
☐ Solitary Vireo †	
☐ Warbling Vireo	
☐ Philadelphia Vireo †	
☐ Red-eyed Vireo	
☐ Tennessee Warbler	
☐ Orange-crowned Warbler	
☐ Nashville Warbler	
☐ Yellow Warbler	
☐ Chestnut-sided Warbler †	
	Jan Feb Mar Apr May Jun Jul Aug Sep Oct Nov Dec

	Jan Feb Mar Apr May Jun Jul Aug Sep Oct Nov Dec
☐ Magnolia Warbler	
☐ Cape May Warbler †	
☐ Black-throated Blue Warbler	
☐ Yellow-rumped Warbler	
☐ Townsend's Warbler †	
☐ Black-throated Green Warbler	
☐ Blackburnian Warbler	
☐ Palm Warbler	
☐ Bay-breasted Warbler	
☐ Blackpoll Warbler	
☐ Black-and–white Warbler	
☐ American Redstart	
☐ Ovenbird	
☐ Northern Waterthrush	
☐ Connecticut Warbler †	
☐ Mourning Warbler	
☐ MacGillivray's Warbler	
☐ Common Yellowthroat	
☐ Wilson's Warbler	
☐ Canada Warbler	
☐ Yellow-breasted Chat †	
☐ Western Tanager	
☐ Rose-breasted Grosbeak	
☐ Black-headed Grosbeak	
☐ Lazuli Bunting †	
☐ Rufous-sided Towhee †	
☐ American Tree Sparrow	
☐ Chipping Sparrow	
	Jan Feb Mar Apr May Jun Jul Aug Sep Oct Nov Dec

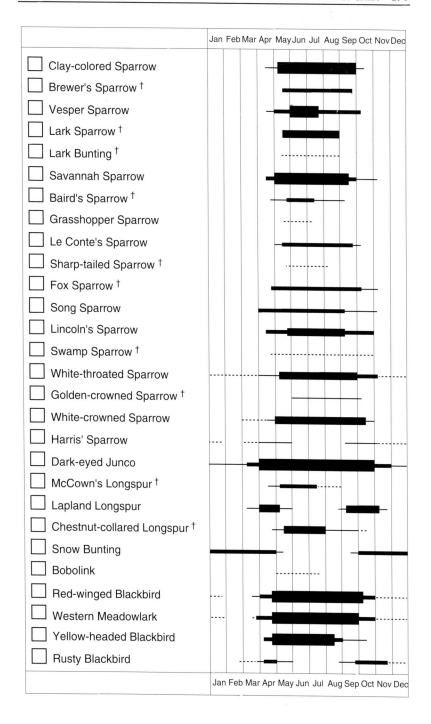

	Jan Feb Mar Apr May Jun Jul Aug Sep Oct Nov Dec
☐ Clay-colored Sparrow	
☐ Brewer's Sparrow †	
☐ Vesper Sparrow	
☐ Lark Sparrow †	
☐ Lark Bunting †	
☐ Savannah Sparrow	
☐ Baird's Sparrow †	
☐ Grasshopper Sparrow	
☐ Le Conte's Sparrow	
☐ Sharp-tailed Sparrow †	
☐ Fox Sparrow †	
☐ Song Sparrow	
☐ Lincoln's Sparrow	
☐ Swamp Sparrow †	
☐ White-throated Sparrow	
☐ Golden-crowned Sparrow †	
☐ White-crowned Sparrow	
☐ Harris' Sparrow	
☐ Dark-eyed Junco	
☐ McCown's Longspur †	
☐ Lapland Longspur	
☐ Chestnut-collared Longspur †	
☐ Snow Bunting	
☐ Bobolink	
☐ Red-winged Blackbird	
☐ Western Meadowlark	
☐ Yellow-headed Blackbird	
☐ Rusty Blackbird	
	Jan Feb Mar Apr May Jun Jul Aug Sep Oct Nov Dec

	Jan Feb Mar Apr May Jun Jul Aug Sep Oct Nov Dec
☐ Brewer's Blackbird	
☐ Common Grackle	
☐ Brown-headed Cowbird	
☐ Northern Oriole	
☐ Rosy Finch [†]	
☐ Pine Grosbeak	
☐ Purple Finch [†]	
☐ Cassin's Finch	
☐ House Finch	
☐ Red Crossbill	
☐ White-winged Crossbill	
☐ Common Redpoll	
☐ Hoary Redpoll	
☐ Pine Siskin	
☐ American Goldfinch	
☐ Evening Grosbeak	
☐ House Sparrow	
☐	
☐	
☐	
☐	
☐	
☐	
☐	
☐	
☐	
☐	
☐	
	Jan Feb Mar Apr May Jun Jul Aug Sep Oct Nov Dec

Rarely-Observed Species

The following species have been reported in the Calgary Region in fewer than five years since 1975. Unless otherwise stated, it should be assumed that these are sight records and that they refer to a single bird. Currently, neither the Calgary Region nor the province of Alberta has an Ornithological Records Committee and no attempt has been made to judge the validity of the sight records given below. This information has been compiled from all known published sources and from records stored at the Inglewood Bird Sanctuary.

Yellow-billed Loon – Oct 27 and Nov 2–5, 1975, first confirmed provincial record; winter of 1976/77; Nov-Dec, 1979; and Oct 13, 1991. Most records are from Glenmore Reservoir (A-6).

Clark's Grebe – May 24, 1988 at Namaka Lake (B-4), first record for the Calgary Region; bred at Namaka Lake in 1992.

Great Egret – June 18–22, 1977 at Frank Lake (B-8), 6th provincial record; May 12, 1980 at Airdrie; and June 15, 1987 at Glenmore Reservoir (A-6).

Snowy Egret – June 19, 1977 at Frank Lake (B-8), 8th provincial record; May 10, 1983 at Bruce Lake (B-6); and May 21, 1989 at Glenmore Reservoir (A-6).

Little Blue Heron – May 19–25, 1991 on slough near Hwy 36 (west of Lake Newell, E-4), photo, first provincial record.

Cattle Egret – June 18, 1980 at High River, 3rd provincial record; and Aug 15–20, 1986 at Strathmore.

Green-backed Heron – Sept 5–9, 1989 and Sept 9-Oct 3, 1990 at Pearce Estate Park (see map A-1); July 4, 1990 at the west end of Glenmore Reservoir (A-6); and several reports between May 30 and June 17, 1992 at Inglewood Bird Sanctuary (A-1).

Brant – Oct 21 and 28, 1984 at Glenmore Reservoir (A-6), first record for the Calgary Region.

Garganey – June 12–15, 1982 near Strathmore, photo; and May 18, 1991 west of Lake Newell (E-4), photo.

Tufted Duck – May 2–6, 1992 at McElroy Slough (B-5), photo, first provincial record.

Yellow Rail – May 31-June 7, 1988 along Sibbald Creek Trail (C-10); and June-July 1990–92 at Big Hill Springs marsh (C-1).

Virginia Rail – Sept 9, 1980, a slightly injured bird taken to, and released at, Inglewood Bird Sanctuary (A-1); May 30, 1982 near Big Hill Springs Provincial Park; July 2–25, 1983 at Twin Lakes (near Kathyrn); and June, 1992 near Olds and June 7-July, 1992 at Pocaterra Marsh (C-11).

Whooping Crane – Sept 19, 1975 flock of 24 near Cochrane; and a single bird Oct 24, 1991 at Balzac.

Spotted Redshank – Sept 19, 1987 at Dalemead Reservoir (B-1), hypothetical for province.

Wandering Tattler – Aug 8, 1988 at Dalemead Reservoir (B-1).

Rufous-necked Stint – Aug 6, 1986 near Shepard, hypothetical for province.

Temminck's Stint – Oct 8, 1990 at Johnson's Island (B-1), hypothetical for province.

Sharp-tailed Sandpiper – Four records for 1990: one near Irricana on Sept 29, first record for the Calgary Region; two birds on Sept 30 and one on Oct 1 at Dalemead Reservoir (B-1); and one on Oct 14 at Eagle Lake (B-3).

Curlew Sandpiper – Oct 9, 1975 at Frank Lake (B-8), photo, first provincial record.

Spoonbill Sandpiper – Two on May 19, 1984 at a slough northwest of Bruce Lake (B-6), hypothetical for province; and one on May 9, 1992 at the same location.

Ruff – Two on July 24, 1982 east of Calgary; one on July 31 and Aug 1, 1982 at Namaka Lake (B-4); two on Aug 13, 1983 at Langdon Slough (B-6); and one Sept 29–30, 1990 at Dalemead Reservoir (B-1).

Long-tailed Jaeger – Aug 17, 1975 at Upper Kananaskis Lake (C-11); and Sept 5, 1982 at Namaka Lake (B-4).

Little Gull – One adult and one 2nd winter on Sept 22–29, 1985 at Eagle (B-3) and Namaka (B-4) lakes, photo, first provincial record; one 2nd winter on Oct 23, 1988 at Namaka Lake; and one juvenile on Oct 24–25, 1991 at Glenmore Reservoir (A-6).

Iceland Gull – May 11, 1986; March 26 and Nov 13, 1988; and April 16, 1990. All at the Inglewood Bird Sanctuary (A-1).

Lesser Black-backed Gull – Five records in 1989, all at the Inglewood Bird Sanctuary (A-1): April 9 and 19; Aug 29; and Sept 5 and 6; photo, first provincial record. Also at I.B.S. on May 7, 1991.

Black-legged Kittiwake – Nov 13, 1976 in northwest Calgary, specimen, first confirmed provincial record; and June 6, 1982 at Bruce Lake (B-6), photo.

Arctic Tern – Sept 11 and 17, 1982 at Namaka Lake (B-4), photo; May 24, 1986 at Longview; and May 24, 1988 at Namaka Lake.

Ancient Murrelet – October 17–20, 1982 at Glenmore Reservoir (A-6), photo, 2nd provincial record.

Black-billed Cuckoo – Four Calgary records: June 11 and Aug 3, 1977; July 16, 1981; and July 1, 1982 at Nose Hill (A-5). Also one bird on July 14–17 and Aug 2, 1982 at Irricana. This species is believed to occur more frequently in the Region than these records suggest.

Common Poorwill – June 5, 1979 at Bow Valley Provincial Park (C-7); and May 31, 1986 at Calgary, specimen.

Vaux's Swift – May 24, 1992 two birds at Mt Allan in the Kananaskis (C-11).

Black-chinned Hummingbird – June 25, 1979 at Calgary, specimen; and June 10, 1989 at Turner Valley.

Anna's Hummingbird – Oct 6–31, 1976 at Calgary, first provincial record; Oct 13-Nov 5, 1977 at Calgary; Aug 20-Sept 27, 1990 at Cremona, photo; and Aug 14-Oct 7, 1991 at Turner Valley, photo. The Calgary and Cremona birds were immature males and the Turner Valley individual an adult male.

Williamson's Sapsucker – June 24, 1992 freshly deceased female found in northeast Calgary; first confirmed provincial record.

Scissor-tailed Flycatcher – Aug 18–22, 1986 near Madden, photo, first confirmed record for the Calgary Region.

Fork-tailed Flycatcher – June 1, 1988 at Drumheller, hypothetical for province.

Purple Martin – Two nesting records with young: 1976 in southwest Calgary, and 1991 at Chestermere.

Chestnut-backed Chickadee – Oct 31, 1981 at Banff Townsite; and two on April 22, 1988 at Bowness Park (A-4).

Sedge Wren – Nov 1, 1985 at Namaka Lake (B-4), first record for the Calgary Region; and May 28, 1992 at Nose Hill Park (A-5).

Blue-gray Gnatcatcher – One at the Inglewood Bird Sanctuary (A-1) from Oct 23-Dec 1, 1987 and Nov 9–22, 1988. Based on behaviour and location (same group of bushes), presumed to be the same individual. Photo; first provincial record.

Northern Wheatear – Nov 22, 1989 on Nose Hill (A-5), photo, first provincial record.

Eastern Bluebird – May 28-June 13, 1977 in southwest Calgary; June 8–16 and Aug 23, 1977 near Millarville; March 30, 1984 at Water Valley; Aug 26, 1985 at Turner Valley; Aug 25, 1986 at Drumheller; and Oct 26, 1986 at Beynon.

Western Bluebird – Two pairs raised double broods in 1985 near Turner Valley. One pair seen at the same location in 1986. A pair was observed over several weeks in June, 1992 at Rafter Six Ranch (near Bow Valley Provincial Park), breeding status unknown.

Northern Mockingbird – June 5, 1988 at Dinosaur Provincial Park (E-2); and late Dec 1990-May 20, 1991 in southwest Calgary.

Sage Thrasher – May 19, 1986 near Keoma, first record for the Calgary Region. Extremely rare and local breeder outside the Region in southeastern Alberta.

Northern Parula – May 15, 1985 at the Inglewood Bird Sanctuary (A-1). First Calgary Region record since specimen from Turner Valley, June 6, 1958.

Black-throated Gray Warbler – Aug 11, 1983 at the Inglewood Bird Sanctuary (A-1); June 11-July 3, 1984 at Bowness Park (A-4); and July 1, 1987 along the Galatea Creek hiking trail (C-11).

Pine Warbler – Sept 1, 1982 at Calgary; Sept 28, 1987 in northwest Calgary; Aug 16, 1991 along Bearspaw Road (off Hwy 1A, northwest of Calgary).

Kentucky Warbler – June 18–21, 1988 in the Weaselhead Natural Area (A-6), photo, first provincial record.

Scarlet Tanager – Aug 1, 1982 at the Inglewood Bird Sanctuary (A-1); May 30, 1985 at Lowery Gardens (A-3); and Nov 13 and 18, 1987 in northwest Calgary.

Northern Cardinal – May 22–23, 1987 at Water Valley, photo, first provincial record.

Indigo Bunting – July 8, 1981 at Trap Creek (C-12); July 18–23, 1983 at Turner Valley; June 29, 1984 at the Highwood River Group Camp (C-12); and July 15, 1988 at North Glenmore Park (A-6).

Dickcissel – May 26, 1982 near Cremona. First record for the Calgary Region since one near Brooks in 1972.

Reporting of Bird Sightings

Documentation of bird sightings is the basis for the "Seasonal Status and Abundance Chart" and "Species Locator" found in this Guide. It is important that birders continue to record their observations and to make them available for use in the production of new checklists as well as for publications such as this one. Calgary area records since the 1970s are stored at a central location and are readily accessible to researchers.

A sample form for reporting unusual sightings has been included for your guidance and use. You may copy this or obtain blank forms (together with copies of the CFNS Bird Record Sheet for regularly sighted species) by contacting:

> City of Calgary
> Inglewood Bird Sanctuary #63
> PO Box 2100, Station M
> Calgary, Alberta, T2P 2M5
>
> Telephone: (403) 237–8821

When reporting an unusual sighting, as well as the completed form, please enclose your original field notes (or a photocopy of them) and a detailed sketch. This should indicate shape, plumage characteristics and any unique features. A photograph or colour slide would be welcomed for rare species.

Record Form for
Unusual Bird Sightings

Species: Date seen:

Number: Age: Sex:

Locality (exact information if possible):

Time: Length of time observed:

Observer(s):

Who first identified the bird?

Are you certain of the identification?   Are Others?

Was a field guide used while the bird was under observation?

If so, how did it influence your decision?

Distance from bird:

Optical equipment used:

Weather/light conditions:

Was the bird photographed?   By whom:

Previous experience with the species:

Description (plumage, behaviour, voice and/or call notes etc.):

Habitat:

Comparison species present:

How were similar species eliminated:

Your name & address:

Date of report preparation: Signature:

Useful Books

Alberta Wildlife Viewing Guide. Edmonton: Lone Pine Publishing, 1990. *This guide to the major wildlife viewing sites of Alberta includes several of interest to birders.*

Ealey, David M. and Martin K. McNichol. A Bibliography of Alberta Ornithology. (2nd ed.) Natural History Occasional Paper No. 16. Edmonton: Provincial Museum of Alberta, 1991. *A computerized listing of over 7,000 Albertan ornithological references.*

Elphinstone, Dave. Inglewood Bird Sanctuary—A Place for all Seasons. Calgary: Rocky Mountain Books, 1990.

Gadd, Ben. Handbook of the Canadian Rockies. Jasper: Corax Press, 1986. *An informative book on the natural history and geology of the Rocky Mountains and foothills of Alberta. The chapter on wilderness safety is particularly recommended.*

Godfrey, W. Earl. The Birds of Canada. (Rev. ed.) Ottawa: National Museum of Natural Sciences, 1986. *The definitive reference on Canadian birds.*

Pinel, H.W., W.W. Smith and C.R. Wershler. Alberta Birds 1971–1980. Vol.1. Non-Passerines. Natural History Occasional Paper No. 13. Edmonton: Provincial Museum of Alberta, 1991.

Pinel, H.W., W.W. Smith and C.R. Wershler. Alberta Birds 1971–1980. Vol.2. Passerines. Natural History Occasional Paper. Edmonton: Provincial Museum of Alberta (In press). *These two volumes analyze provincial data and include information on migration, range extensions, significant breeding and winter records, population changes and habitat preferences.*

Salt, W.R. and J.R. Salt. The Birds of Alberta. Edmonton: Hurtig, 1978. *A valuable, if slightly dated, source of information on Alberta birds.*

Van Tighem, Kevin. Birding Jasper National Park. Jasper: Parks and People, 1988.

Identification aids:-

Clark, William S. <u>Hawks</u>. Peterson Field Guide Series No. 35. Boston: Houghton Mifflin Company, 1987.

Grant, P.J. <u>Gulls: A Guide to Identification</u>. (2nd ed.) London: T. & A.D. Poyser, 1986.

Hayman, Peter, John Marchant and Tony Prater. <u>Shorebirds: An Identification Guide</u>. Boston: Houghton Mifflin Company, 1986.

Kaufman, Kenn. <u>A Field Guide to Advanced Birding</u>. Peterson Field Guide Series No. 39. Boston: Houghton Mifflin Company, 1990. *Most of this excellent book on identification problems is pertinent to southern Alberta.*

Madge, Steve and Hilary Burn. <u>Waterfowl: An Identification Guide to the Ducks, Geese and Swans of the World</u>. Boston: Houghton Mifflin Company, 1988.

National Geographic Society. <u>Field Guide to the Birds of North America</u>. (2nd ed.) Washington: 1987.

Peterson, Roger Tory. <u>A Field Guide to Western Birds</u>. (3rd ed.) Peterson Field Guide Series No. 2. Boston: Houghton Mifflin Company, 1990.

Robbins, Chandler S., Bertel Bruun and Herbert S. Zim. <u>Birds of North America</u>. (Rev. ed.) New York: Golden Press, 1983.

Aids to getting around:-

Bullick, Terry. <u>Calgary Parks and Pathways</u>. Calgary: Rocky Mountain Books,1990.

Daffern, Gillean. <u>Kananaskis Country Trail Guide</u>. Calgary: Rocky Mountain Books,1985.

Dodd, John and Gail Helgason. <u>The Canadian Rockies Access Guide</u>. Edmonton: Lone Pine Publishing,1991.

Index

A

Alberta Special Crops & Horti-
cultural Research Centre 154
Avocet:
American 50, 53, 66, 69, 140

B

Badlands Trail 146
Bankside 14
Barrier Lake 109
Bassano Dam 143
Beaver Pond Picnic Area 110
Beaverdam Flats Natural Area 35
Bebo Grove 13, 14
Big Hill Springs Provincial Park 72
Bittern:
American 50, 58, 66, 122, 156, 158,
159
Blackbird:
Brewer's 14, 23, 62, 117
Red-winged 14, 56, 66, 77, 103,
105, 117, 122, 150
Rusty 35, 37, 97, 122
Yellow-headed 56, 66, 69, 74, 77,
150, 153
Bluebird:
Eastern 184
Mountain 28, 32, 62, 63, 86, 88, 96,
97, 102, 117, 133, 145
Western 185
Bobolink 58
Boulton Creek 114
Bow Valley Provincial Park 94
Bowness Park 18
Brant 181
Brown-Lowery Recreation Area 91
Bruce Lake 56
Bufflehead 35, 36, 57, 94, 98, 112

Buller Mountain Picnic Area 101
Bunting:
Indigo 185
Lark 146, 167
Lazuli 23, 117, 167
Snow 24, 32, 54, 85, 118, 126, 146
Burnsmead 14

C

Canvasback 66, 103
Canyon Day Use Area 113
Carburn Park 36
Cardinal:
Northern 185
Carseland Weir 42
Catbird:
Gray 13, 17, 18, 23, 27, 63, 72, 145,
147
Cave and Basin Marsh 121
Chat:
Yellow-breasted 62, 145, 147, 167
Chickadee:
Black-capped 10, 20, 27, 35, 61, 89,
96, 122
Boreal 14, 15, 20, 27, 83, 89, 93, 96,
106, 112, 122, 125, 130, 133
Chestnut-backed 18, 184
Mountain 14, 15, 83, 86, 89, 90, 96,
106, 118, 119, 130, 133, 136, 138
Consolation Lakes Trail 137
Coot:
American 66, 103, 140, 150
Cormorant:
Double-crested 21, 33, 45, 56, 140,
142, 150, 153, 156
Cottonwood Flats Trail 146
Cowbird:
Brown-headed 150

Crane:
    Sandhill 47, 51, 54, 67, 83
    Whooping 182
Crawling Valley Recreation Area 142
Crawling Valley Reservoir 142
Creeper:
    Brown 17, 20, 27, 35, 90, 93, 96,
    122, 125, 130
Crossbill:
    Red 17, 27, 30, 82, 85, 105, 106,
    109, 118
    White-winged 17, 20, 27, 30, 85,
    93, 96, 101, 102, 118, 125, 130, 133,
    138
Crow:
    American 32, 136
Cuckoo:
    Black-billed 183
Curlew:
    Long-billed 39, 53, 55, 67, 140,
    146, 150

D
Dalemead Reservoir 41
Dawson Hiking Trail 105
Death Valley Hiking Trail 89
Dickcissel 185
Dinosaur Provincial Park 143
Dipper:
    American 14, 72, 85, 90, 96, 98, 99,
    110, 113, 114, 117, 122, 125, 126,
    127, 134, 165
Dogpound Creek 81
Douglas Fir Trail 15
Dove:
    Mourning 27, 59, 63, 86, 150
Dowitcher:
    Long-billed 45, 51, 53, 58
    Short-billed 45

Duck:
    Harlequin 10, 35, 36, 90, 110, 112,
    114, 117, 134, 160
    Ring-necked 57, 74, 80, 83, 94, 97,
    102, 103, 112, 113
    Ruddy 66
    Tufted 53, 182
    Wood 10, 84, 160
Dunlin 45, 51, 58

E
Eagle:
    Bald 10, 14, 33, 35, 36, 37, 47, 51,
    67, 72, 75, 78, 82, 88, 89, 94, 96, 98,
    103, 109, 113, 115, 126, 145, 161
    Golden 67, 69, 75, 82, 85, 88, 89,
    101, 103, 107, 109, 110, 115, 118,
    133, 140, 145, 161
Eagle Lake 46
Eagle Lake Park 48
Egret:
    Cattle 181
    Great 181
    Snowy 56, 181
Evan-Thomas Creek 110

F
Falcon:
    Peregrine 89, 133, 142, 161
    Prairie 23, 31, 33, 62, 69, 72, 77, 81,
    89, 94, 115, 132, 140, 145, 147, 156
Fenland Trail 124
Finch:
    Cassin's 110
    Purple 14, 27, 78, 168
    Rosy 85, 89, 101, 119, 132, 133, 168
Fish Creek Provincial Park 11, 37
Flicker:
    Northern 10, 13, 27, 35, 37, 86, 102
Flowing Water Trail 96

Flycatcher:
    Alder 23, 27, 80, 96, 105, 110, 117, 122, 125, 126
    Cordilleran 165
    Dusky 13, 85, 86, 90, 97, 110, 117, 165
    Fork-tailed 62, 184
    Hammond's 129, 164
    Least 10, 13, 27, 63, 72, 96, 110, 117, 150
    Olive-sided 14, 27, 85, 90, 101, 102, 106, 118, 122, 137
    Pacific-slope 165
    Scissor-tailed 184
    Western 14, 82, 85, 86, 90, 99, 105, 110, 113, 117, 118, 128, 137, 165
    Willow 27, 96, 97, 105, 110, 114, 118, 122, 125, 130, 164
    Yellow-bellied 88
Forest Lawn Pond 51
Forest Management Interpretive Trail 109
Forestry Trunk Road 83
Fortress Mountain Ski Area 110
Frank Lake 64

G
Gadwall 14, 35, 36, 66
Galatea Creek 110
Garganey 156, 182
Ghost Reservoir 85
Glenmore Reservoir 24
Glenmore Trail Bridge 36
Gnatcatcher:
    Blue-gray 10, 184
Godwit:
    Hudsonian 45, 51, 53, 142
    Marbled 50, 53, 66, 140, 146, 150
Golden-Plover:
    Lesser 39, 45, 51, 142, 157

Goldeneye:
    Barrow's 10, 36, 58, 74, 94, 96, 97, 102, 103, 112, 113, 126, 161
    Common 10, 14, 27, 35, 57, 97, 98, 101
Goldfinch:
    American 23, 96, 117, 150
Goose:
    Canada 14, 17, 36, 42, 45, 53, 66, 74, 77, 103, 150
    Greater White-fronted 45, 47, 51, 53, 67, 69, 142, 160
    Ross' 67, 69, 160
    Snow 51, 67, 69, 142, 160
Goshawk:
    Northern 14, 17, 20, 23, 28, 32, 33, 78, 89, 93, 105, 106, 110, 118
Grackle:
    Common 57, 150, 154
Grand Valley Road 75, 82
Grass Pass Hiking Trail 117
Grassi Lakes 99
Grebe:
    Clark's 159, 181
    Eared 45, 47, 66, 94, 140, 150
    Horned 45, 66, 74, 150
    Pied-billed 45, 66, 74, 103, 150
    Red-necked 45, 74, 94, 126, 142, 150
    Western 45, 67, 150
Grosbeak:
    Evening 17, 78, 83, 93, 96, 125
    Pine 20, 27, 31, 61, 90, 93, 125, 133, 138
    Rose-breasted 14, 17, 20, 31, 78, 146
Grouse:
    Blue 85, 89, 114, 127, 130, 162
    Ruffed 14, 27, 72, 78, 86, 89, 97, 105, 112, 118

Sharp-tailed 21, 61, 82
Spruce 85, 89, 90, 102, 106, 109, 112, 113, 114, 118, 129, 130, 132
Gull:
  Bonaparte's 51, 57, 142
  California 50, 57, 142, 150, 156
  Franklin's 50, 66, 150, 158
  Glaucous 10, 51, 98
  Glaucous-winged 10, 51
  Herring 51, 57
  Iceland 10, 183
  Lesser Black-backed 10, 183
  Little 47, 51, 183
  Mew 10
  Ring-billed 20, 30, 50, 57, 142, 150, 156
  Sabine's 47, 51
  Thayer's 10
Gyrfalcon 14, 23, 28, 33, 35, 51, 77, 81, 94, 161

H
Harrier:
  Northern 50, 54, 66, 133, 140, 146, 150
Hawk:
  Cooper's 20, 33, 57, 89, 93, 126, 133, 142
  Ferruginous 59, 61, 140, 145, 146, 151, 156, 161
  Red-tailed 13, 18, 23, 32, 33, 36, 51, 54, 59, 70, 81, 89, 105, 107, 115, 133
  Rough-legged 23, 33, 51, 54, 75, 78, 81, 94, 115
  Sharp-shinned 10, 17, 89, 110, 113, 117, 133, 137, 142
  Swainson's 13, 23, 32, 50, 51, 54, 58, 62, 66, 67, 70, 81, 86, 107, 115, 133, 140, 146

Heron:
  Black-crowned Night- 33, 50, 56, 66, 69, 140, 150, 153, 154, 156, 159
  Great Blue 13, 35, 36, 50, 56, 73, 140, 150
  Green-backed 181
  Little Blue 156, 181
Highwood House 118
Highwood Pass 118
Highwood River Group Camp 117
Horseshoe Canyon 61
Hull's Wood 14
Hummingbird:
  Anna's 184
  Black-chinned 184
  Calliope 96, 97, 112, 118, 164
  Ruby-throated 27, 154, 164
  Rufous 26, 27, 72, 96, 97, 110, 112, 114, 117, 118, 127, 164

I
Ibis:
  White-faced 74, 158, 159
Inglewood Bird Sanctuary 8, 33

J
Jaeger:
  Long-tailed 183
  Parasitic 47, 51, 98
Jamieson Lake 153
Jay:
  Blue 14, 15, 18, 20, 78, 83
  Gray 14, 78, 83, 86, 90, 93, 102, 105, 112, 125, 130, 132, 136, 138
  Steller's 90, 102, 109, 110, 118, 134, 136
John Peake Memorial Park 53
Johnson Lake 153
Johnson's Island 42
Johnston Canyon 127

Junco:
   Dark-eyed 14, 88, 97, 101, 102, 122, 133, 138
Junction Creek Picnic Area 90

K

Kananaskis Canyon Interpretive Trail 113
Keoma 56
Kestrel:
   American 10, 13, 23, 32, 62, 77, 81, 86, 145
Killdeer 14, 20, 35, 37, 50, 66, 97, 122, 140, 150
Kinbrook Island Provincial Park 148
King Creek Day Use Area 110
Kingbird:
   Eastern 10, 13, 50, 57, 117, 150
   Western 62, 150, 153, 165
Kingfisher:
   Belted 13, 20, 27, 35, 37, 73, 97, 112, 122
Kinglet:
   Golden-crowned 15, 20, 90, 93, 112, 122, 125, 130, 133, 136, 138
   Ruby-crowned 14, 15, 85, 93, 96, 112, 122, 125, 130, 133, 136, 138, 150
Kininvie Marsh 158
Kitsim Reservoir 156
Kittiwake:
   Black-legged 57, 183
Knot:
   Red 67, 157

L

Lac Des Arcs 98
Lake Louise 134
Lake McGregor Recreation Area 67
Lake Newell 148, 156

Langdon Slough 56
Lantern Creek Trail 118
Lark:
   Horned 23, 50, 54, 67, 105, 133, 140, 146, 151
Laryx-Grizzly Lake Loop 133
Longspur:
   Chestnut-collared 41, 59, 67, 140, 151, 157, 168
   Lapland 51, 54
   McCown's 59, 67, 140, 150, 151, 156, 157, 158, 168
Loon:
   Common 51, 53, 56, 74, 98, 101, 102, 114, 133, 142, 150, 153
   Pacific 26, 86, 159
   Red-throated 26, 47, 159
   Yellow-billed 26, 181
Lower Kananaskis Lake 114
Lowery Gardens 17

M

Mallard 10, 103, 122
Mallard Point 14
Many Springs Trail 97
Marl Lake Interpretive Trail 113
Martin:
   Purple 150, 184
McElroy Slough 53
McGregor Lake 67
McMullen Island Picnic Area 62
Meadowlark:
   Western 23, 26, 50, 55, 66, 86, 96, 140, 146
Merganser:
   Common 10, 13, 14, 20, 35, 57, 101, 117, 133
   Hooded 10, 26, 36, 57, 74, 80, 83, 98, 112, 122, 126, 161
   Red-breasted 10, 26, 57, 161

Merlin 17, 23, 28, 31, 33, 37, 133,
    140, 154
Mockingbird:
    Northern 145, 185
Moraine Lake 137
Mount Engadine Lodge 102
Mt Allan Viewpoint 109
Mt Indefatigable Trail 114
Mud Lake 102
Muleshoe Picnic Area 129
Murrelet:
    Ancient 26, 183

N
Namaka Lake 49
Night-Heron:
    Black-crowned 33, 50, 56, 66, 69,
    140, 150, 153, 154, 156, 159
Nighthawk:
    Common 145, 164
North Ghost Recreation Area 85
Nose Hill Park 21
Nutcracker:
    Clark's 90, 102, 118, 119, 126, 130,
    132, 136, 138, 165
Nuthatch:
    Red-breasted 14, 20, 27, 30, 93, 125,
    130, 133, 136, 138, 150
    White-breasted 10, 35, 37, 93

O
Oldsquaw 26, 33, 37, 47, 51, 86, 160
Onetree Reservoir 153
Oriole:
    Northern 10, 13, 17, 27, 117, 145,
    150
Osprey 21, 28, 89, 96, 97, 98, 102,
    126, 161
Ovan's Slough 77
Ovenbird 13, 80, 97

Owl:
    Barred 13, 80, 83, 93, 104, 105, 125,
    163
    Boreal 80, 93, 105, 110, 112, 125,
    163
    Burrowing 39, 140, 151, 154, 156,
    158, 163
    Great Gray 80, 83, 85, 88, 93, 104,
    105, 163
    Great Horned 10, 13, 14, 20, 27,
    35, 36, 51, 54, 57, 61, 80
    Long-eared 23
    Northern Hawk 77, 80, 81, 82, 85,
    90, 94, 163
    Northern Pygmy- 14, 80, 83, 85,
    88, 104, 105, 106, 110, 125, 163
    Northern Saw-whet 14, 20, 35, 72,
    80, 93, 105, 163
    Short-eared 23, 39, 56, 63, 67, 80,
    154
    Snowy 39, 47, 52, 69, 80, 146, 154,
    163

P
Partridge:
    Gray 17, 23, 32, 35, 37, 50, 54, 61,
    70
Parula:
    Northern 10, 185
Pelican:
    American White 42, 50, 56, 69,
    142, 143, 150, 153, 159
Peter Lougheed Provincial Park 107
Phalarope:
    Red 51, 162
    Red-necked 45, 51
    Wilson's 50, 53, 58, 66, 73, 140, 150
Pheasant:
    Ring-necked 13, 23, 35, 37, 54, 57,
    61

Phoebe:
    Eastern 13, 27, 72, 96, 117
    Say's 62, 145, 165
Pine Grove Group Camp 105
Pintail:
    Northern 14, 35, 66
Pipit:
    American 51, 54, 118, 119, 133
    Sprague's 23, 55, 58, 59, 66, 67, 74,
    140, 166
Plain of Six Glaciers Trail 134
Plover:
    Black-bellied 45, 51, 53, 142, 153,
    156, 157
    Lesser Golden- 39, 45, 51, 142, 157
    Piping 162
    Semipalmated 45, 51, 133
Pocaterra Trail 112
Poorwill:
    Common 183
Pothole Creek 94
Ptarmigan:
    White-tailed 118, 132, 133, 162
Ptarmigan Cirque 118
Pygmy-Owl:
    Northern 14, 80, 83, 85, 88, 104,
    105, 106, 110, 125, 163

Q
Quarry Road Trail 17

R
Rail:
    Virginia 182
    Yellow 74, 105, 182
Railway Slough 58
Raven:
    Common 14, 96, 102, 105, 106,
    118, 126, 130, 132, 136
Redhead 14, 36, 66

Redpoll:
    Common 14, 20, 30, 35, 37, 96,
    125, 126
Redshank:
    Spotted 41, 182
Redstart:
    American 10, 17, 72, 122, 125, 130,
    145, 150
River Swamp Trail 124
Robin:
    American 136
Rock Isle Lake Loop Trail 132
Rosebud River 62
Royal Tyrrell Museum of
    Palaeontology 61
Ruff 41, 183

S
Sadler's Slough 44
Sanderling 45, 53
Sandpiper:
    Baird's 45, 51, 53
    Buff-breasted 47, 51
    Curlew 182
    Least 45, 51, 53
    Pectoral 20, 45, 51, 53, 142
    Semipalmated 45, 51, 53
    Sharp-tailed 41, 182
    Solitary 13, 45, 73, 80, 101, 133,
    138
    Spoonbill 57, 182
    Spotted 13, 20, 27, 63, 73, 96, 102,
    107, 112, 117, 133, 138, 150
    Stilt 45, 51, 142
    Upland 41, 48, 58, 66, 74, 162
    Western 45
    White-rumped 45, 56
Sapsucker:
    Red-naped 72, 80, 86, 89, 93, 102,
    106, 117, 164

Williamson's 184
Yellow-bellied 13, 26, 80, 105, 106, 117
Scandia Recreation Area 157
Scaup:
    Greater 26, 51, 58, 114, 160
    Lesser 35, 36, 66
Scoter:
    Black 26, 47, 109, 160
    Surf 26, 58, 74, 86, 98, 109, 126, 161
    White-winged 26, 53, 58, 74, 86
Seebe Pond 98
Shannon Terrace 14
Sheep River Falls Picnic Area 90
Sheep River Wildlife Sanctuary 86
Shepard 39
Shoveler:
    Northern 66
Shrike:
    Loggerhead 55, 140, 145, 146, 166
    Northern 24, 28, 32, 55, 77, 82, 88
Sibbald Flats 105
Silver Creek Park 82
Siskin:
    Pine 14, 17, 20, 27, 30, 72, 78, 88, 93, 97, 101, 102, 105, 117, 125, 133, 136, 138, 153
Snipe:
    Common 35, 37, 48, 50, 56, 66, 73, 74, 77, 96, 105, 112, 118, 122, 150
Solitaire:
    Townsend's 32, 54, 86, 90, 96, 101, 102, 114, 118, 128, 130, 132, 138
Sora 13, 27, 39, 47, 48, 50, 57, 66, 73, 77, 80, 96, 103, 105, 150
South Glenmore Natural Area 27
Sparrow:
    American Tree 37, 78
    Baird's 23, 50, 56, 57, 58, 64, 66, 74, 167

Brewer's 101, 110, 133, 146, 167
Chipping 13, 31, 88, 101, 102, 117, 118
Clay-colored 13, 17, 18, 23, 26, 31, 53, 55, 72, 86, 96, 117, 146
Fox 31, 106, 110, 118, 130, 133, 136, 137, 138, 168
Golden-crowned 133, 168
Grasshopper 26, 56
Lark 63, 145, 147, 167
Le Conte's 13, 17, 23, 27, 31, 50, 57, 74, 105
Lincoln's 13, 17, 20, 23, 31, 102, 112, 117, 118, 125, 126
Savannah 13, 23, 26, 31, 50, 53, 54, 66, 96, 117, 122
Sharp-tailed 73, 167
Song 17, 20, 72, 117, 118, 122, 125, 126
Swamp 105, 110, 168
Vesper 23, 26, 31, 50, 53, 55, 72, 86, 96, 117, 146
White-crowned 20, 30, 31, 101, 102, 110, 117, 118, 122, 125, 133
White-throated 13, 20, 30, 31, 102, 105, 146, 150
Springbank 77
Stilt:
    Black-necked 39, 56, 66, 157, 158
Stint:
    Rufous-necked 39, 182
    Temminck's 182
Stoney Trail 110
Strawberry Campground Marsh 118
Sullivan Creek 117
Sunshine Meadows 130
Swallow:
    Bank 13, 17, 62, 98
    Barn 13, 98, 107, 132, 136
    Cliff 13, 15, 62, 63, 98, 103, 107, 118, 136, 145

Northern Rough-winged 13, 17, 98, 107
Tree 13, 75, 98, 107
Violet-green 97, 98, 99, 130, 136, 145, 165
Swan:
Trumpeter 14, 26, 33, 84, 88, 94, 103, 126, 159
Tundra 26, 33, 51, 53, 57, 58, 63, 67, 98, 103, 126, 142
Swen Bayer Peninsula Wildlife Reserve 150
Swift:
Black 110, 112, 128, 164
Vaux's 110, 183

T

Tanager:
Scarlet 185
Western 14, 17, 20, 31, 72, 88, 90
Tattler:
Wandering 41, 182
Teal:
Blue-winged 13, 66
Cinnamon 45, 66, 73, 126, 160
Green-winged 35, 37, 66, 122
Tern:
Arctic 51, 183
Black 15, 50, 57, 66, 69, 74, 94, 103, 107, 150
Caspian 51, 53
Common 15, 47, 50, 57, 69, 126, 142, 150, 156
Forster's 47, 50, 57, 66, 163
Thrasher:
Brown 23, 27, 62, 145, 147
Sage 57, 185
Thrush:
Hermit 80, 90, 93, 101, 110, 118, 130, 132, 133, 137

Swainson's 62, 80, 85, 90, 93, 96, 99, 101, 106, 112, 125, 132, 150
Varied 85, 90, 93, 101, 102, 105, 110, 112, 113, 118, 125, 130, 132, 133, 136, 138, 165
Tillebrook Provincial Park 154
Towhee:
Rufous-sided 18, 27, 62, 145, 167
Trans-Canada/Sibbald Creek Trail pond 103
Trap Creek 117
Turkey:
Wild 162
Turnstone:
Ruddy 51, 67, 156, 157

U

University of Calgary Campus 28
Upper Kananaskis Lake 114

V

Veery 13, 15, 27, 93, 150
Vermilion Lakes Drive 125
Vermilion Lakes Overlook 126
Vireo:
Philadelphia 166
Red-eyed 10, 13, 86, 126
Solitary 80, 88, 93, 166
Warbling 10, 13, 96, 117, 126, 145, 150
Votier's Flats 13
Vulture:
Turkey 61, 161

W

Warbler:
Bay-breasted 10, 17, 18
Black-and–white 10, 17, 145
Black-throated Blue 10, 82
Black-throated Gray 10, 18, 185

Black-throated Green 10, 17
Blackburnian 17
Blackpoll 10, 30, 72, 145, 150, 154
Canada 10, 17
Cape May 10, 17, 93, 167
Chestnut-sided 10, 17, 96, 166
Connecticut 17, 80, 167
Kentucky 27, 185
MacGillivray's 10, 17, 31, 72, 90, 106, 112, 117, 118, 126
Magnolia 10, 17
Mourning 17
Nashville 10, 17, 82, 97
Orange-crowned 10, 17, 20, 30, 72, 114, 122, 125, 126, 145
Palm 10, 17
Pine 185
Tennessee 10, 13, 17, 20, 30, 72, 88, 93, 117, 126
Townsend's 10, 17, 93, 101, 110, 122, 125, 129, 130, 133, 136, 166
Wilson's 10, 17, 20, 30, 80, 97, 102, 106, 112, 114, 117, 118, 122, 125, 126, 130, 133, 137
Yellow 10, 13, 17, 27, 30, 57, 62, 63, 72, 86, 96, 105, 117, 118, 126, 150
Yellow-rumped 10, 15, 17, 30, 57, 85, 88, 90, 93, 97, 99, 101, 102, 114, 117, 125, 129, 133, 136, 138, 150
Water Valley 81
Waterthrush:
Northern 17, 27, 30, 72, 81, 90, 96, 112, 117, 118, 126, 130
Waxwing:
Bohemian 17, 20, 30, 31, 35, 61, 85, 93, 101, 102
Cedar 13, 18, 27, 63, 72, 86, 102, 150
Weaselhead Natural Area 26
Wheatear:
Northern 24, 184

Wigeon:
American 13, 14, 35, 66, 98, 122
Eurasian 53, 58, 59, 69, 84, 98, 160
Willet 50, 66, 69, 140, 150
William J. Bagnall Wilderness Park 82
Winchell Lake 83
Windy Point 89
Wolf Lake 140
Wood-Pewee:
Western 10, 13, 17, 27, 72, 96, 117, 145, 150
Woodpecker:
Black-backed 20, 90, 91, 102, 164
Downy 13, 17, 35, 37, 61, 93, 102
Hairy 13, 17, 86, 93, 102
Lewis' 117
Pileated 14, 61, 62, 80, 82, 89, 93, 105, 118, 125, 127, 130, 145
Three-toed 14, 17, 20, 27, 90, 91, 96, 102, 125, 127, 136, 164
Wren:
House 13, 27, 62, 150
Marsh 48, 50, 57, 66, 150, 153
Rock 23, 62, 145, 147, 165
Sedge 184
Winter 106, 110, 127, 130, 136, 137, 165
Wyndham-Carseland Provincial Park 43

Y
Yellowlegs:
Greater 45, 51
Lesser 45, 51, 105, 107
Yellowthroat:
Common 10, 13, 17, 2'7, 50, 57, 96, 97, 102, 105, 106, 118, 122, 125, 126, 130, 150

Notes

Notes

Notes

Notes